THE CUISINART
BREAD MACHINE
COOKBOOK

250

Hands-Off Bread Making Recipes for Your Cuisinart Bread Maker

AMANDA COOK

Copyright

No part of this publication may be reproduced, stored in a retrieval system or transmitted in any form or by any means, electronic, mechanical, photocopying, recording, scanning or otherwise, except as permitted under Sections 107 or 108 of the 1976 United States Copyright Act, without the prior written permission of the Publisher. Requests to the Publisher for permission should be addressed to the Permissions Department.

Limit of Liability/Disclaimer of Warranty: The Publisher and the author make no representations or warranties with respect to the accuracy or completeness of the contents of this work and specifically disclaim all warranties, including without limitation warranties of fitness for a particular purpose. No warranty may be created or extended by sales or promotional materials. The advice and strategies contained herein may not be suitable for every situation. This work is sold with the understanding that the publisher is not engaged in rendering medical, legal or other professional advice or services.

If professional assistance is required, the services of a competent professional person should be sought. Neither the Publisher nor the author shall be liable for damages arising here from. The fact that an individual, organization or website is referred to in this work as a citation and/or potential source of further information does not mean that the author or the Publisher endorses the information the individual, organization or website may provide or recommendations they/it may make. Further, readers should be aware that Internet websites listed in this work might have changed or disappeared between when this work was written and when it is read.
The author publishes its books in a variety of electronic and print formats. Some content that appears in print may not be available in electronic books, and vice versa.

TRADEMARKS: All other trademarks are the property of their respective owners. The author is not associated with any product or vendor mentioned in this book

Table of Contents

Table of Contents	3
INTRODUCTION	6
Basic Bread	7
Gluten-Free White Bread	7
Oat Bran Molasses Bread	7
Molasses Wheat Bread	8
Italian Bread	8
Baguette Style French Bread	9
100 Percent Whole-Wheat Bread	9
Bread Machine Bread	10
100% Whole Wheat Bread	10
Banana Bread	10
Crusty French Bread	11
Onion Bread	11
Buttermilk Bread	11
Pumpernickel Bread	12
Oat Molasses Bread	12
Grain-Free Chia Bread	13
Fat-Free Whole Wheat Bread	13
Peanut Butter Bread	13
Whole Wheat Corn Bread	14
Multigrain Bread	14
Sunflower and Flax Seed Bread	14
Quinoa Oatmeal Bread	15
Gluten-Free Brown Bread	15
Whole-Wheat Buttermilk Bread	16
Easy Gluten-Free, Dairy-Free Bread	16
Wheat Bran Bread	17
Soft Egg Bread	17
Date and Nut Bread	18
Rye Bread	18
Multi-Seed Bread	18
Healthy Bran Bread	19
Classic Whole Wheat Bread	19
Coffee Rye Bread	21
Dark Rye Bread	21
Honey Nut Bread	22
Oat Bran Nutmeg Bread	22
Three-Seed Bread	23
Peasant Bread	23
English muffin Bread	23
Golden Raisin Bread	24
Multigrain Honey Bread	24
Classic Dark Bread	25
Classic Corn Bread	25
Traditional Italian Bread	26
Basic Seed Bread	26
Double-Chocolate Zucchini Bread	27
Basic Bulgur Bread	27
Oat Quinoa Bread	28
SOURDOUGH BREADS	29
Basic Honey Bread	29
Multigrain Sourdough Bread	29
Onion Buttermilk Bread	30
Faux Sourdough Bread	30
Pecan Cranberry Bread	31
Sourdough Milk Bread	31
Cheese Potato Bread	32
Lemon Sourdough Bread	32
FRUIT BREADS	34
Cranberry & Golden Raisin Bread	34
Zucchini Bread	34
Cinnamon Figs Bread	36
Robust Date Bread	36
Cranberry Honey Bread	37
Apple Spice Bread	37
Poppy Seed–Lemon Bread	38
Ginger-Carrot-Nut Bread	38
Orange Bread	39
Lemon-Lime Blueberry Bread	39
Honey Banana Bread	40
Banana Whole-Wheat Bread	40
Oatmeal-Streusel Bread	41
Garlic Olive Bread	42

Brown Bread with Raisins	42
Cinnamon Pumpkin Bread	43
Plum Orange Bread	43
Blueberries 'n Orange Bread	44
Peaches and Cream Bread	44
Gluten-Free Glazed Lemon-Pecan Bread	45
Fresh Blueberry Bread	45
Gluten-Free Best-Ever Banana Bread	46
SPICE AND NUT BREAD	**47**
Cardamom Honey Bread	47
Cracked Black Pepper Bread	47
Pistachio Cherry Bread	48
Herb and Garlic Cream Cheese Bread	48
Mix Seed Raisin Bread	50
Grain, Seed And Nut Bread	50
Honey-Spice Egg Bread	52
Anise Honey Bread	52
Basic Pecan Bread	53
Apple Walnut Bread	53
Simple Garlic Bread	54
Herbed Pesto Bread	54
Caraway Rye Bread	55
Anise Lemon Bread	55
Fragrant Cardamom Bread	56
Chocolate Mint Bread	56
Molasses Candied-Ginger Bread	57
Whole-Wheat Seed Bread	57
Multigrain Bread	58
Pecan Raisin Bread	58
Toasted Pecan Bread	59
Quinoa Oatmeal Bread	59
Market Seed Bread	60
Pesto Nut Bread	60
Cracked Wheat Bread	61
Double Coconut Bread	61
Seed Bread	62
Honeyed Bulgur Bread	62
Chia Seed Bread	63
Flaxseed Honey Bread	63
Chia Sesame Bread	64

Sesame French Bread	64
Quinoa Whole-Wheat Bread	65
Peanut Butter Bread	65
Toasted Hazelnut Bread	66
VEGETABLE BREAD	**67**
Potato Honey Bread	67
Mashed Potato Bread	67
Dilly Onion Bread	68
Onion Chive Bread	68
Basil Tomato Bread	69
Confetti Bread	69
Honey Potato Flakes Bread	70
Pretty Borscht Bread	70
Zucchini Lemon Bread	71
Yeasted Pumpkin Bread	71
Oatmeal Zucchini Bread	72
Hot Red Pepper Bread	72
French Onion Bread	73
Golden Butternut Squash Raisin Bread	73
Sweet Potato Bread	74
CHEESE BREADS	**75**
Jalapeno Cheddar Bread	75
Oregano Cheese Bread	75
Cheddar Cheese Basil Bread	76
Spinach and Feta Bread	76
Blue Cheese Bread	77
Parsley Garlic Bread	77
Prosciutto Parmesan Breadsticks	78
Jalapeño Corn Bread	78
Cheddar Bacon Bread	79
Italian Cheese Bread	79
Olive Cheese Bread	80
Cheesy Sausage Loaf	80
Mixed Herb Cheese Bread	81
Blue Cheese Onion Bread	81
Cheddar and Bacon Bread	82
Basil Cheese Bread	82
Double Cheese Bread	83
American Cheese Beer Bread	83

Mozzarella and Salami Bread	84
Simple Cottage Cheese Bread	84
SWEET BREAD	**85**
Swedish Coffee Bread	85
Pear Kuchen with Ginger Topping	85
Walnut Cocoa Bread	86
Sweet Applesauce Bread	86
Mexican Chocolate Bread	88
Sour Cream Maple Bread	88
Chocolate Chip Bread	89
Milk Sweet Bread	89
Barmbrack Bread	89
Pumpernickel Bread	91
Allspice Currant Bread	91
Apple Butter Bread	92
Beer and Pretzel Bread	92
Buttermilk Pecan Bread	93
Crusty Honey Bread	93
Brown Sugar Date Nut Swirl Bread	94
Cashew Butter/Peanut Butter Bread	94
Honey Granola Bread	95
Delicious Sour Cream Bread	95
Black Bread	96
Apple Cider Bread	96
Sweet Pineapple Bread	97
Coffee Cake	98
Caramel Apple and Pecan Bread	98
Cocoa Banana Bread	99
Pumpkin Coconut Bread	99
Cranberry-Cornmeal Bread	100
Coconut Delight Bread	100
Vanilla Almond Milk Bread	101
Chocolate Chip Bread	101
Triple Chocolate Bread	102

Sweet Vanilla Bread	103
Chocolate Oatmeal Banana Bread	103
SPECIALTY BREAD	**104**
Festive Raspberry Rolls	104
Italian Easter Cake	104
Eggnog Bread	105
Basil Pizza Dough	105
Whole-Wheat Challah	106
Classic Sourdough Bread	106
Portuguese Sweet Bread	107
Milk Honey Sourdough Bread	107
Pecan Maple Bread	108
Cherry Christmas Bread	108
Nana's Gingerbread	109
Coffee Caraway Seed Bread	109
Bread Machine Brioche	110
Sun-Dried Tomato Rolls	110
Cinnamon Beer Bread	111
Traditional Paska	111
French Butter Bread	112
Raisin and Nut Paska	112
Holiday Chocolate Bread	113
Honey Cake	113
New Year Spiced Bread	114
Christmas Fruit Bread	114
Cocoa Holiday Bread	115
Stollen	115
Holiday Eggnog Bread	116
Julekake	116
Easter Bread	117
Spiked Eggnog Bread	117
Hot Buttered Rum Bread	118
Zucchini Pecan Bread	118
About the Author	**119**

INTRODUCTION

The CUISINART Bread Machine Cookbook: Hands-Off Bread Making Recipes for Your Cuisinart Bread Maker.

Congratulations! This is a valuable acquisition for any home. With our Cuisinart Bread Machine Cookbook, you can serve your family with hot bread and fragrant pastries every day.

The Cuisinart Bread Machine Cookbook will be the only book and guide you need to help you easily bake the most mouthwatering loaves of bread every time, regardless if you are a beginner or seasoned baker.

The Cuisinart Bread Machine Cookbook: The Best, Easy, Gluten-Free, and Foolproof recipes for your Cuisinart Bread Machine.

There is nothing better than the exquisite and delicious aroma of freshly baked bread that fills the kitchen. However, baking bread from scratch is a slow, challenging, and complicated process.

Having to knead, taste, and bake the dough can take hours, and creating the perfect rise and crispy increase can take years to master. When it comes to baking bread at home from scratch, things can get tricky. Thankfully, that's where The Cuisinart Bread Machine Cookbook for Beginners comes in!

Everyone loves the taste and smell of the fresh bread, but not the time it takes to bake it. Making bread should be simple... and now it is. The Cuisinart Bread machine is now the hot item in the kitchen because it takes the work out of making homemade bread. Even better, The Cuisinart Bread Machine Cookbook takes the mystery out of the Cuisinart Bread Machine and brings you easy-to-use recipes.

The Cuisinart Bread Machine Cookbook is an assortment of techniques, tips, tricks, and near and dear recipes that were collected throughout the years and wishes to share with you now.

With more than 250 recipes that use easy-to-find ingredients and require minimal work, this Cuisinart Bread Machine Cookbook will set you up for baking success.

Put down the dough and pick up this book. The Cuisinart Bread Machine Cookbook is the first and only collection of easy, hassle-free recipes that give you delicious homemade loaves of bread every time.

The best sweet bread machine recipes in this Cuisinart bread machine recipe cookbook allow you to create healthy breads with a conventional kitchen appliance.

I test each Cuisinart bread machine recipe in this bread machine cookbook, and all the tips for improving bread are taken from my own experience.

There's nothing than the taste and smell of homemade bread!

Enjoy The Cuisinart Bread Machine Cookbook!

Gluten-Free White Bread
PREP: 10 MINUTES OR LESS/ MAKES 1 LOAF

Ingredients
2 eggs
1⅓ cups milk
6 Tbsp oil
1 tsp vinegar
3⅝ cups white bread flour
1 tsp salt
2 Tbsp sugar
2 tsp dove farm quick yeast

Directions
1. **Preparing the Ingredients.** Add each ingredient to the Cuisinart Bread Machine in the order and at the temperature recommended by manufacturer.
2. **Select the Bake cycle.** Close and start the machine on the gluten free bread Set, if available. Alternatively use the basic or rapid setting with a dark crust option. When the Cuisinart Bread Machine has finished baking, remove the bread and put it on a cooling rack.

Oat Bran Molasses Bread
PREP: 10 MINUTES / MAKES 1 LOAF

Ingredients
Water - ½ cup
Melted butter - 1½ tbsp., cooled
Blackstrap molasses - 2 tbsp.
Salt - ¼ tsp.
Ground nutmeg - ⅛ tsp.
Oat bran - ½ cup
Whole-wheat bread flour - 1½ cups
Bread machine or instant yeast - 1⅛ tsp.

Directions
1. **Preparing the Ingredients**
   Place the ingredients in the Cuisinart Bread Machine according to instructions.
2. **Select the Bake cycle**
   Choose Whole-Wheat/Whole-Grain bread, and Light or Medium crust. Press Start. Remove when done and cool. Slice and serve.

Molasses Wheat Bread
PREP: 10 MINUTES OR LESS/MAKES 1 LOAF

Ingredients
12 slice bread (1½ pound)
- ¾ cup water, at 80°F to 90°F
- ⅓ cup milk, at 80°F
- 1 tablespoon melted butter, cooled
- 3¾ tablespoons honey
- 2 tablespoons molasses
- 2 teaspoons sugar
- 2 tablespoons skim milk powder
- ¾ teaspoon salt
- 2 teaspoons unsweetened cocoa powder
- 1¾ cups whole-wheat flour
- 1¼ cups white bread flour
- 1⅛ teaspoons bread machine yeast or instant yeast

Directions
1. **Preparing the Ingredients.**
   Choose the size of bread to prepare. Measure and add the ingredients to the pan in the order as indicated in the ingredient listing. Insert the bread pan in the Cuisinart Bread Machine.
2. **Select the Bake cycle**
   Press the "Start" button. Select the White / Basic setting, then select the dough size and crust color. Press start to start the cycle.
   When this is done, and the bread is baked, remove the pan from the machine. Let stand a few minutes.
   Take the bread out. Leave it on a wire rack to cool for at least 10 minutes.
   After this time, proceed to cut it.

Italian Bread
PREP: 10 MINUTES OR LESS/MAKES 1 LOAF

Ingredients
- Water - ⅔ cup
- Olive oil - 1 tbsp.
- Sugar - 1 tbsp.
- Salt - ¾ tsp.
- White bread flour - 2 cups
- Bread machine or instant yeast - 1 tsp.

Directions
1. **Preparing the Ingredients**
   Add everything in the Cuisinart Bread Machine according to instructions.
2. **Select the Bake cycle**
   Select Basic/White bread and Light or Medium crust. Press Start.
   When done, remove the bread. Cool, slice, and serve.

Baguette Style French Bread
PREP: 10 MINUTES OR LESS/MAKES 1 LOAF

Ingredients
8 slice bread (1 pound)
2 baguettes of 1-pound each
1 ⅔ cups water, lukewarm between 80 and 90°F
1 teaspoon table salt 4 ⅔ cups white bread flour
2 ⅔ teaspoons bread machine yeast or rapid rise yeast
2 baguettes of ¾-pound each
12 slice bread (1½ pound)
¾ cup water, at 80°F to 90°F
1 ¼ cups water, lukewarm between 80 and 90°F
¾ teaspoon table salt
3 ½ cups white bread flour
2 teaspoons bread machine yeast or rapid rise yeast

Directions
1. **Preparing the Ingredients.**
   Choose the size of crusty bread you would like to make and measure your ingredients. Add the ingredients for the Cuisinart Bread Machine to the bread pan in the order listed above. Insert the bread pan in the Cuisinart Bread Machine. Press the "Start" button.
2. **Select the Bake cycle**
   Select the dough/manual setting. When the dough cycle is completed, remove the pan and lay the dough on a floured working surface. Knead the dough a few times and add flour if needed so the dough is not too sticky to handle. Cut the dough in half and form a ball with each half. Grease a baking sheet with olive oil. Dust lightly with cornmeal. Preheat the oven to 375° and place the oven rack in the middle position. With a rolling pin dusted with flour, roll one of the dough balls into a 12-inch by 9 -inch rectangle for the 2 pounds bread size or a 10-inch by 8-inch rectangle for the 1 ½ pound bread size. Starting on the longer side, roll the dough tightly. Pinch the ends and the seam with your fingers to seal. Roll the dough in a back in forth movement to make it into a nice French baguette shape. Repeat the process with the second dough ball. Place loaves of bread onto the baking sheet with the seams down and brush with some olive oil with enough space in between them to rise. Dust top of both loaves with a little bit of cornmeal. Cover with a clean kitchen towel and place in a warm area with any air draught. Let rise for 10 to 15 minutes, or until loaves doubled in size. Mix the egg white and 1 tablespoon of water and lightly brush over both loaves of bread. Place in the oven and bake for 20 minutes. Remove from oven and brush with remaining egg wash on top of both loaves of bread. Place back into the oven taking care of turning around the baking sheet. Bake for another 5 to 10 minutes or until the baguettes are golden brown. Let rest on a wired rack for 5-10 minutes before serving.

100 Percent Whole-Wheat Bread
PREP: 10 MINUTES OR LESS/MAKES 1 LOAF

Ingredients
12 slice bread (1½ pound)
  1⅛ cups water, at 80°F to 90°F
  2¼ tablespoons melted butter, cooled
  2¼ tablespoons honey
  1⅛ teaspoons salt
  3 cups whole-wheat bread flour
  2 teaspoons sugar
  2 tablespoons skim milk powder
  ¾ teaspoon salt
  1½ teaspoons bread machine or instant yeast

Directions
1. **Preparing the Ingredients.**
   Choose the size of bread to prepare. Measure and add the ingredients to the pan in the order as indicated in the ingredient listing. Insert the bread pan in the Cuisinart Bread Machine.
2. **Select the Bake cycle**
   Press the "Start" button. Select the Wheat/ Whole setting, then select the dough size and crust color. Press start to start the cycle. When this is done, and the bread is baked, remove the pan from the machine. Let stand a few minutes.
   Take the bread out. Leave it on a wire rack to cool for at least 10 minutes. Slice and serve.

Bread Machine Bread
PREP: 10 MINUTES / MAKES 1 LOAF

Ingredients
Flour – 2 cups, sifted
Warm water – ¾ cup
Sugar – 1 tsp.
Active dry yeast – 1.25 tsp.
Salt – 1 tsp.
Oil – 1 tsp.

Directions
1. **Preparing the Ingredients**
   Add ingredients according to bread machine recommendation.
2. **Select the Bake cycle**
   Select the Basic setting and press Start. Remove the loaf once it is baked. Cool and slice.

100% Whole Wheat Bread
PREP: 10 MINUTES / MAKES 1 LOAF

Ingredients
16 slice bread (2 pound)
   1¼ cups lukewarm water
   2 tablespoons vegetable oil or olive oil
   ¼ cup honey or maple syrup
   1½ teaspoons table salt
   3½ cups whole wheat flour
   ¼ cup sesame, sunflower, or flax seeds (optional)
   1½ teaspoons bread machine yeast

Directions
1. **Preparing the Ingredients.**
   Choose the size of loaf you would like to make and measure your ingredients. Add the ingredients to the bread pan in the order listed above. Insert the bread pan in the Cuisinart Bread Machine.
2. **Select the Bake cycle**
   Press the "Start" button. Select the Whole Wheat/Wholegrain setting, then select the dough size and crust color. Press start to start the cycle.
   When this is done, and the bread is baked, remove the pan from the machine. Let stand a few minutes.
   Take the bread out. Leave it on a wire rack to cool for at least 10 minutes.
   After this time, proceed to cut it.

Banana Bread
PREP: 10 MINUTES / MAKES 1 LOAF

Ingredients
Eggs – 2
Butter – 1/3 cup
Milk – 1/8 cup
Bananas – 2, mashed
Bread flour – 1 1/3 cups
Sugar – 2/3 cup
Baking powder – 1 ¼ tsp.
Baking soda – ½ tsp.
Salt – ½ tsp.
Chopped nuts – ½ cup, lightly toasted

Directions
1. **Preparing the Ingredients**
   Add the butter, eggs, milk, and bananas to the bread pan and set aside. Combine the remaining dry ingredients in a bowl and add the bread pan.
2. **Select the Bake cycle**
   Use Quick Bread setting to bake the bread. Take the bread out. Leave it on a wire rack to cool for at least 10 minutes. Slice and serve.

Crusty French Bread
PREP: 10 MINUTES / MAKES 1 LOAF

Ingredients
12 slice bread (1½ pound)
1 cup water, at 80°F to 90°F
1¼ tablespoons olive oil
2 tablespoons sugar
1¼ teaspoons salt
3 cups white bread flour
1¼ teaspoons bread machine or instant yeast, or flax seeds (optional)

Directions
1. **Preparing the Ingredients.**
   Place the ingredients in your bread maker as recommended by the manufacturer.
2. **Select the Bake cycle**
   Set the machine for French bread, select light or medium crust, and press Start.
   When this is done, and the bread is baked, remove the pan from the machine. Let stand a few minutes.
   Take the bread out. Leave it on a wire rack to cool for at least 10 minutes.

Onion Bread
PREP: 10 MINUTES / MAKES 1 LOAF

Ingredients
Water – 1 ½ cup
Butter – 2 tbsp. plus 2 tsp.
Salt – 1 tsp.
Sugar – 1 tbsp. plus 1 ½ tsp.
Bread flour – 4 cups
Nonfat dry milk – 2 tbsp. plus 2 tsp.
Active dry yeast – 2 tsp.
Dry onion soup mix – 4 tbsp.

Directions
1. **Preparing the Ingredients**.
   Place ingredients in the bread pan in the order listed, except the soup.
2. **Select the Bake cycle**
   Select Basic cycle. Add the onion soup mix at the fruit and nut signal.
   When done, remove and cool. Slice and serve.

Buttermilk Bread
PREP: 10 MINUTES / MAKES 1 LOAF

Ingredients
16 slice bread (2 pounds)
1¼ cups lukewarm buttermilk
1½ tablespoons unsalted butter, melted
1½ tablespoons sugar
1⅛ teaspoons table salt
⅓ teaspoon baking powder
2⅔ cups white bread flour
1⅔ teaspoons bread machine yeast

Directions
1. **Preparing the Ingredients**.
   Choose the size of bread to prepare. Measure and add the ingredients to the pan in the order as indicated in the ingredient listing. Insert the bread pan in the Cuisinart Bread Machine.
2. **Select the Bake cycle**
   Close, Press the "Start" button. Select the White / Basic setting, then select the dough size and crust color. Press start to start the cycle.
   When this is done, and the bread is baked, remove the pan from the machine. Let stand a few minutes.
   Take the bread out. Leave it on a wire rack to cool for at least 10 minutes. Slice and serve.

Pumpernickel Bread

PREP: 10 MINUTES / MAKES 1 LOAF

Ingredients

8 slice bread (1½ pounds)
½ cup water, at 80°F to 90°F
¼ cup brewed coffee, at 80°F to 90°F
2 tablespoons dark molasses
5 teaspoons sugar
4 teaspoons melted butter, cooled
1 tablespoon powdered skim milk
1 teaspoon salt
⅔ cup dark rye flour
½ cup whole-wheat bread flour
1 teaspoon caraway seeds
1 cup white bread flour
1½ teaspoons bread machine or active dry yeast

Directions

1. **Preparing the Ingredients.**
   Place the ingredients in your bread maker as recommended by the manufacturer.
2. **Select the Bake cycle**
   Close, Press the "Start" button. Select the White / Basic setting, then select the dough size and crust color. Press start to start the cycle.
   When this is done, and the bread is baked, remove the pan from the machine. Let stand a few minutes.
   Take the bread out. Leave it on a wire rack to cool for at least 10 minutes. Slice and serve.

Oat Molasses Bread

PREP: 10 MINUTES / MAKES 1 LOAF

Ingredients

12 slice bread (1½ pounds)
1 cup boiling water
⅓ cup brewed coffee, at 80°F to 90°F
2 tablespoons butter
1 large egg, lightly beaten
3 cups white bread flour
1½ teaspoons table salt
3 tablespoons honey
1 tablespoon dark molasses
3 cups white bread flour
2 teaspoons bread machine yeast

Directions

1. **Preparing the Ingredients.**
   Add the boiling water and oats to a mixing bowl. Allow the oats to soak well and cool down completely. Do not drain the water. Choose the size of loaf you would like to make and measure your ingredients Add the soaked oats, along with any remaining water, to the bread pan. Add the remaining ingredients to the bread pan in the order listed above.
2. **Select the Bake cycle**
   Close, Press the "Start" button. Select the White / Basic setting, then select the dough size and crust color. Press start to start the cycle.
   When this is done, and the bread is baked, remove the pan from the machine. Let stand a few minutes.
   Take the bread out. Leave it on a wire rack to cool for at least 10 minutes. Slice and serve.

Grain-Free Chia Bread
PREP: 5 MINUTES / MAKES 12

Ingredients
1 cup warm water
3 large organic eggs, room temperature
1/4 cup olive oil
1 tablespoon apple cider vinegar
1 cup gluten-free chia seeds, ground to flour
1 cup almond meal flour
1/2 cup potato starch
1/4 cup coconut flour
3/4 cup millet flour
1 tablespoon xanthan gum
1 1/2 teaspoons salt
2 tablespoons sugar
3 tablespoons nonfat dry milk
6 teaspoons instant yeast

Directions
1. **Preparing the Ingredients.**
   Whisk wet ingredients together and add to the bread maker pan.
   Whisk dry ingredients, except yeast, together and add on top of wet ingredients.
   Make a well in the dry ingredients and add yeast.
2. **Select the Bake cycle**
   Select Whole Wheat cycle, light crust color, and press Start.
   Allow to cool completely before serving.

Fat-Free Whole Wheat Bread
PREP: 10 MINUTES / MAKES 1 LOAF

Ingredients
Water – 1 7/8 cup
White whole wheat flour – 4 2/3 cups
Vital wheat gluten – 4 tbsp.
Sugar – 2 tbsp.
Salt – 1 ½ tsp.
Rapid rise yeast – 2 ½ tsp.

Directions
1. **Preparing the Ingredients.**
   Add the water in the Cuisinart Bread Machine pan. Add the remaining ingredients according to bread machine recommendation.
2. **Select the Bake cycle**
   Choose Quick-Bake Whole Wheat cycle and press Start. Remove the bread when complete. Cool, slice, and serve.

Peanut Butter Bread
PREP: 10 MINUTES / MAKES 1 LOAF

Ingredients
Water – 1 cup, plus 1 tbsp.
Peanut butter – ½ cup
Bread flour – 3 cups
Brown sugar – 3 tbsp.
Salt – 1 tsp.
Bread machine yeast – 2 tsp.

Directions
1. **Preparing the Ingredients**
   Place every ingredient in the Cuisinart Bread Machine according to the manufacturer's recommendation.
2. **Select the Bake cycle**
   Select Basic/White or Sweet and choose Medium or Light crust. Press Start. Remove the bread when finished. Cool, slice, and serve.

Whole Wheat Corn Bread
PREP: 10 MINUTES /MAKES 1 LOAF

Ingredients
16 slice bread (2 pounds)
1⅓ cups lukewarm water
2 tablespoons light brown sugar
1 large egg, beaten
2 tablespoons unsalted butter, melted
1½ teaspoons table salt
¾ cup whole wheat flour
¾ cup cornmeal
3 cups whole-wheat bread flour
2¾ cups white bread flour
2½ teaspoons bread machine yeast

Directions
1. **Preparing the Ingredients.** Measure and add the ingredients to the pan in the order mentioned above. Insert the bread pan in the Cuisinart Bread Machine.
2. **Select the Bake cycle.** Press the "Start" button. Select the White / Basic setting, then select the dough size and crust color. Press start to start the cycle. When this is done, and the bread is baked, remove the pan from the machine. Let stand a few minutes. Take the bread out. Leave it on a wire rack to cool for at least 10 minutes.
After this time, proceed to cut it

Multigrain Bread
PREP: 10 MINUTES /MAKES 1 LOAF

Ingredients
Water – 1 ¼ cups
Butter – 2 tbsp. softened
Bread flour – 1 1/3 cups
Whole wheat flour – 1 1/3 cups
Seven grain or multigrain cereal – 1 cup
Brown sugar – 3 tbsp.
Salt – 1 ¼ tsp.
Bread machine yeast – 2 ½ tsp.

Directions
1. **Preparing the Ingredients.** Place everything in the Cuisinart Bread Machine pan according to bread machine recommendation.
2. **Select the Bake cycle.** Press the "Start" button. Select the White / Basic or Whole Wheat setting, then select the dough size and crust color. Press start to start the cycle. When this is done, and the bread is baked, remove the pan from the machine. Let stand a few minutes. Take the bread out. Leave it on a wire rack to cool for at least 10 minutes. Slice and serve.

Sunflower and Flax Seed Bread
PREP: 10 MINUTES /MAKES 1 LOAF

Ingredients
Water – 1 1/3 cups
Butter – 2 tbsp., softened
Honey – 3 tbsp.
Bread flour – 1 ½ cups
Whole wheat bread flour – 1 1/3 cups
Salt – 1 tsp.
Active dry yeast – 1 tsp.
Flax seeds – ½ cup
Sunflower seeds – ½ cup

Directions
1. **Preparing the Ingredients**
Place everything (except sunflower seeds) in the Cuisinart Bread Machine according to machine recommendation.
2. **Select the Bake cycle**

Select Basic White cycle and press Start. Add the seeds after the alert sounds. Cool, slice, and serve.

Quinoa Oatmeal Bread
PREP: 10 MINUTES / MAKES 1 LOAF

Ingredients

Quinoa flakes – ½ cup
Buttermilk – 1 cup
Salt – 1 tsp.
Sugar – 1 tbsp.
Honey – 1 tbsp.
Unsalted butter – 4 tbsp.
Quick-cooking oats – ½ cup
Whole wheat flour – ½ cup
Bread flour – 1 ½ cups
Yeast – 1 ½ tsp.

Directions

1. **Preparing the Ingredients.**
   Add everything according to the Cuisinart Bread Machine instructions.

2. **Select the Bake cycle**
   Select Whole Grain and bake. Remove the bread when done. Cool, slice, and serve.

Gluten-Free Brown Bread
PREP: 5 MINUTES / MAKES 12

Ingredients

2 large eggs, lightly beaten
1 3/4 cups warm water
3 tablespoons canola oil
1 cup brown rice flour
3/4 cup oat flour
1/4 cup tapioca starch
1 1/4 cups potato starch
1 1/2 teaspoons salt
2 tablespoons brown sugar
2 tablespoons gluten-free flaxseed meal
1/2 cup nonfat dry milk powder
2 1/2 teaspoons xanthan gum
3 tablespoons psyllium, whole husks
2 1/2 teaspoons gluten-free yeast for bread machines

Directions

1. **Preparing the Ingredients**
   Add the eggs, water and canola oil to the bread maker pan and stir until combined.
   Whisk all of the dry ingredients except the yeast together in a large mixing bowl.
   Add the dry ingredients on top of the wet ingredients.
   Make a well in the center of the dry ingredients and add the yeast.
2. **Select the Bake cycle**
   Set Gluten-Free cycle, medium crust color, and press Start.
   When the bread is done, lay the pan on its side to cool before slicing to serve.

Whole-Wheat Buttermilk Bread
PREP: 10 MINUTES /MAKES 1 LOAF

Ingredients

12 slice bread (1½ pounds)
¾ cup plus 3 tablespoons buttermilk, at 80°F to 90°F
1½ tablespoons melted butter, cooled
1½ tablespoons honey
¾ teaspoon salt
1⅛ cups whole-wheat flour
1¾ cups plus
1 tablespoon white bread flour
1⅔ teaspoons bread machine or instant yeast

Directions
1. **Preparing the Ingredients.**
   Place the ingredients in your bread maker as recommended by the manufacturer.
2. **Select the Bake cycle**
   Close. Press the "Start" button. Select the White / Basic or Whole Wheat setting, then select the dough size and crust color. Press start to start the cycle.
   When this is done, and the bread is baked, remove the pan from the machine. Let stand a few minutes.
   Take the bread out. Leave it on a wire rack to cool for at least 10 minutes. Slice and serve.

Easy Gluten-Free, Dairy-Free Bread
PREP: 15 MINUTES /MAKES 12

Ingredients

1 1/2 cups warm water
2 teaspoons active dry yeast
2 teaspoons sugar
2 eggs, room temperature
1 egg white, room temperature
1 1/2 tablespoons apple cider vinegar
4 1/2 tablespoons olive oil
3 1/3 cups multi-purpose gluten-free flour

Directions
1. **Preparing the Ingredients**
   Add the yeast and sugar to the warm water and stir to mix in a large mixing bowl; set aside until foamy, about 8 to 10 minutes.
   Whisk the 2 eggs and 1 egg white together in a separate mixing bowl and add to baking pan of bread maker.
   Add apple cider vinegar and oil to baking pan.
   Add foamy yeast/water mixture to baking pan.
   Add the multi-purpose gluten-free flour on top.
2. **Select the Bake cycle**
   Set for Gluten-Free bread setting and Start.
   Remove and invert pan onto a cooling rack to remove the bread from the baking pan. Allow to cool completely before slicing to serve.

Wheat Bran Bread
PREP: 10 MINUTES /MAKES 1 LOAF

Ingredients
16 slice bread (2 pounds)
1½ cups lukewarm milk
3 tablespoons unsalted butter, melted
2 teaspoons table salt
½ cup wheat bran
3½ cups white bread flour
1½ cups whole-wheat bread flour
1 cup oat bran
3 cups whole-wheat bread flour
2 teaspoons bread machine yeast

Directions
1. **Preparing the Ingredients.**
   Measure and add the ingredients to the pan in the order mentioned above. Insert the bread pan in the Cuisinart Bread Machine.
2. **Select the Bake cycle**
   Press the "Start" button. Select the White / Basic or Whole Wheat setting, then select the dough size and crust color. Press start to start the cycle.
   When this is done, and the bread is baked, remove the pan from the machine. Let stand a few minutes.
   Take the bread out. Leave it on a wire rack to cool for at least 10 minutes. Slice and serve.

Soft Egg Bread
PREP: 10 MINUTES /MAKES 1 LOAF

Ingredients
16 slice bread (2 pounds)
1 cup milk, at 80°F to 90°F
5 tablespoons melted butter, cooled
3 eggs, at room temperature
⅓ cup sugar
2 teaspoons salt
4 cups white bread flour
1 cup oat bran
3 cups whole-wheat bread flour
1½ teaspoons bread machine or instant yeast

Directions
1. **Preparing the Ingredients.**
   Place the ingredients in your bread maker as recommended by the manufacturer.
2. **Select the Bake cycle**
   Press the "Start" button. Select the White / Basic setting, then select the dough size and medium crust. Press Start.
   When this is done, and the bread is baked, remove the pan from the machine. Let stand a few minutes.
   Take the bread out. Leave it on a wire rack to cool for at least 10 minutes. Slice and serve.

Date and Nut Bread
PREP: 10 MINUTES /MAKES 1 LOAF

Ingredients
Water – 1 cup
Oil – 1 ½ tbsp.
Honey – 2 tbsp.
Salt – ½ tsp.
Rolled oats – ¾ cup
Whole wheat flour – ¾ cup
Bread flour – 1 ½ cups
Active dry yeast – 1 ½ tsp.
Dates – ½ cups, pitted and chopped
Chopped almonds – ½ cup

Directions
1. **Preparing the Ingredients**
   Place everything into the bread pan according to the Cuisinart Bread Machine recommendation.
2. **Select the Bake cycle**
   Select Fruit bread/Basic cycle and press Start. You can add the dates and nuts after the beep or at the very beginning.

Rye Bread
PREP: 10 MINUTES /MAKES 1 LOAF

Ingredients
16 slice bread (2 pounds)
1⅔ cups lukewarm water
¼ cup + 4 teaspoons Dijon mustard
2 tablespoons unsalted butter, melted
4 teaspoons sugar
1 teaspoon table salt
2 cups rye flour
2⅔ cups white bread flour
1½ teaspoons bread machine yeast

Directions
1. **Preparing the Ingredients.**
   Measure and add the ingredients to the pan in the order mentioned above. Insert the bread pan in the Cuisinart Bread Machine.
   Select the Bake cycle
   Press the "Start" button. Select the White / Basic or Whole Wheat setting, then select the dough size and crust color. Press start to start the cycle.
   When this is done, and the bread is baked, remove the pan from the machine. Let stand a few minutes.
   Take the bread out. Leave it on a wire rack to cool for at least 10 minutes. Slice and serve.

Multi-Seed Bread
PREP: 10 MINUTES /MAKES 1 LOAF

Ingredients
Tepid water – 1 cup
Salt – 1 tsp.
Olive oil – 2 tbsp.
Whole wheat bread flour – 1 cup
White bread flour – 2 cups
Dried yeast – 1 ½ tsp.
Mixed seeds – 1/3 cup sesame, pumpkin, sunflower, poppy

Directions
1. **Preparing the Ingredients.**
   Add the ingredients according to bread machine recommendation.
2. **Select the Bake cycle**
   Select White bread/Basic cycle and press Start. Remove the bread when done. Cool, slice, and serve.

Healthy Bran Bread

PREP: 10 MINUTES /MAKES 1 LOAF

Ingredients

12 slice bread (1½ pounds)
1⅛ cups milk, at 80°F to 90°F
2¼ tablespoons melted butter, cooled
1½ tablespoons unsalted butter, melted
3 tablespoons sugar
1½ teaspoons salt
½ cup wheat bran
2⅔ cups white bread flour
1½ teaspoon bread machine or instant yeast

Directions

1. **Preparing the Ingredients.**
   Measure and add the ingredients to the pan in the order mentioned above. Insert the bread pan in the Cuisinart Bread Machine.
2. **Select the Bake cycle**
   Press the "Start" button. Select the White / Basic or Whole Wheat setting, then select the dough size and crust color. Press start to start the cycle.
   When this is done, and the bread is baked, remove the pan from the machine. Let stand a few minutes.
   Take the bread out. Leave it on a wire rack to cool for at least 10 minutes. Slice and serve.

Classic Whole Wheat Bread

PREP: 10 MINUTES /MAKES 1 LOAF

Ingredients

12 slice bread (1½ pounds)
1⅛ cups milk, at 80°F to 90°F
2¼ tablespoons melted butter, cooled
1½ tablespoons unsalted butter, melted
3 tablespoons sugar
1½ teaspoons salt
½ cup wheat bran
¾ cup lukewarm water
⅓ cup unsalted butter, melted
2 eggs, at room temperature
1½ teaspoons table salt
3 tablespoons sugar
1 cup whole-wheat flour
2 cups white bread flour
1⅔ teaspoons bread machine yeast

Directions

1. **Preparing the Ingredients.**
   Measure and add the ingredients to the pan in the order mentioned above. Insert the bread pan in the Cuisinart Bread Machine.

2. **Select the Bake cycle**
   Press the "Start" button. Select the Whole Wheat setting, then select the dough size and crust color. Press start to start the cycle.
   When this is done, and the bread is baked, remove the pan from the machine. Let stand a few minutes.
   Take the bread out. Leave it on a wire rack to cool for at least 10 minutes. Slice and serve.

Coffee Rye Bread
PREP: 10 MINUTES / MAKES 1 LOAF

Ingredients

Lukewarm water – ½ cup
Brewed coffee – ¼ cup, 80ºF
Dark molasses – 2 tbsp.
Brown sugar – 5 tsp.
Unsalted butter – 4 tsp., softened
Powdered skim milk – 1 tbsp.
Kosher salt – 1 tsp.
Unsweetened cocoa powder – 4 tsp.
Dark rye flour – 2/3 cup
Whole-wheat bread machine flour – ½ cup
Caraway seeds – 1 tsp.
White bread machine flour – 1 cup
Bread machine yeast – 1 ½ tsp

Directions
1. **Preparing the Ingredients**
   Place everything in the Cuisinart Bread Machine pan according to the Cuisinart Bread Machine recommendation.
2. **Select the Bake cycle**
   Select Basic and Light crust. Press Start. Remove the bread. Cool, slice, and serve.

Dark Rye Bread
PREP: 10 MINUTES / MAKES 1 LOAF

Ingredients

12 slice bread (1½ pounds)
1 cup water, at 80°F to 90°F
1½ tablespoons melted butter, cooled
1½ tablespoons unsalted butter, melted
⅓ cup molasses
⅓ teaspoon salt
1½ tablespoons unsweetened cocoa powder
Pinch ground nutmeg
¾ cup rye flour
2 cups white bread flour
1⅔ teaspoons bread machine or instant yeast

Directions
1. **Preparing the Ingredients.**
   Place the ingredients in your bread maker as recommended by the manufacturer.

2. **Select the Bake cycle**
   Press the "Start" button. Select the White / Basic setting, then select the dough size and crust color. Press start to start the cycle.
   When this is done, and the bread is baked, remove the pan from the machine. Let stand a few minutes.
   Take the bread out. Leave it on a wire rack to cool for at least 10 minutes. Slice and serve.

Honey Nut Bread
PREP: 10 MINUTES / MAKES 1 LOAF

Ingredients
Eggs – 2
Cottage cheese – 2/3 cup
Milk – ½ cup
Butter – ¼ cup
Honey – 2 tbsp.
All-purpose flour – 4 cups
Instant yeast – 1 tbsp.
Salt – 1 tsp.
Candied nuts – ¾ cups, chopped

Directions
1. **Preparing the Ingredients**
   Add everything, except nuts to your bread machine according to manufacturer recommendation.
2. **Select the Bake cycle**
   Select Basic and choose Light crust type. Press Start. Add the nuts when the machine beeps. Remove the bread when ready. Cool, slice, and serve.

Oat Bran Nutmeg Bread
PREP: 10 MINUTES / MAKES 1 LOAF

Ingredients
16 slice bread (2 pounds)
1 cup lukewarm water
3 tablespoons unsalted butter, melted
¼ cup blackstrap molasses
½ teaspoon table salt
3 cups whole-wheat bread flour
¼ teaspoon ground nutmeg
1 cup oat bran
3 cups whole-wheat bread flour
2¼ teaspoons bread machine yeast

Directions
1. **Preparing the Ingredients.**
   Choose the size of bread to prepare. Measure and add the ingredients to the pan in the order as indicated in the ingredient listing. Insert the bread pan in the Cuisinart Bread Machine.
2. **Select the Bake cycle**
   Press the "Start" button. Select the White / Basic setting, then select the dough size and crust color. Press start to start the cycle. When this is done, and the bread is baked, remove the pan from the machine.
   Let stand a few minutes.
   Take the bread out. Leave it on a wire rack to cool for at least 10 minutes. Slice and serve.

Three-Seed Bread
PREP: 10 MINUTES / MAKES 1 LOAF

Ingredients
Water – 2/3 cup plus 2 tsp.
Butter – 1 tbsp., softened
Honey – 1 tbsp.
Sunflower seeds – 2 tbsp.
Sesame seeds – 2 tbsp.
Poppy seeds – 2 tbsp.
Salt – ¾ tsp.
Whole wheat flour – 1 cup
Bread flour - 1 cup
Nonfat dry milk powder – 3 tbsp.
Active dry yeast – 2 tsp.

Directions
1. **Preparing the Ingredients**
   Put all ingredients in the Cuisinart Bread Machine pan according to its order.
2. **Select the Bake cycle**
   Select Basic bread and press Start. Remove the bread when done. Cool, slice, and serve.

Peasant Bread
PREP: 10 MINUTES / MAKES 12 SLICES

Ingredients
2 tablespoons full rounded yeast
2 cups white bread flour
1 1/2 tablespoons sugar
1 tablespoon salt
7/8 cup water
For the topping:
Olive oil
Poppy seeds

Directions
1. **Preparing the Ingredients**
   Add water first, then add the dry ingredients to the Cuisinart Bread Machine, reserving yeast.
   Make a well in the center of the dry ingredients and add the yeast.
2. **Select the Bake cycle**
   Choose French cycle, light crust color, and push Start. When bread is finished, coat the top of loaf with a little olive oil and lightly sprinkle with poppy seeds. Allow to cool slightly and serve warm with extra olive oil for dipping.

English muffin Bread
PREP: 10 MINUTES / MAKES 1 LOAF

Ingredients
12 slice bread (1½ pounds)
1¼ cups buttermilk, at 80°F to 90°F
1½ tablespoons melted butter, cooled
1½ tablespoons sugar
1⅛ teaspoons salt
⅓ teaspoon baking powder
2⅔ cups white bread flour
1⅔ teaspoons bread machine or instant yeast

Directions
1. **Preparing the Ingredients.**
   Place the ingredients in your bread maker as recommended by the manufacturer
2. **Select the Bake cycle**
   Close, Press the "Start" button. Select the White / Basic setting, then select the dough size, select light or medium crust. Press start to start the cycle. When this is done, and the bread is baked, remove the pan from the machine. Let stand a few minutes. Remove the bread from the skillet and leave it on a wire rack to cool for at least 10 minutes. Slice and serve.

Golden Raisin Bread
PREP: 10 MINUTES / MAKES 1 LOAF

Ingredients

8 slice bread (pounds)

¾ cup milk, at 80°F to 90°F

1 tablespoon melted butter, cooled

¼ cup molasses

1 tablespoon sugar

¾ teaspoon salt

2 cups white bread flour

1 teaspoon bread machine or instant yeast

½ cup golden raisins

12 slice bread (1½ pounds)

1⅛ cups milk, at 80°F to 90°F

1½ tablespoons melted butter, cooled

Directions
1. **Preparing the Ingredients.**
   Place the ingredients, except the raisins, in your bread machine as recommended by the manufacturer.
2. **Select the Bake cycle**
   Set the machine for Basic/White or Sweet bread, select light or medium crust, and press Start. Add the raisins at the raisin/nut signal. When the bread is done, remove the bucket from the machine.
   Let the loaf cool for 5 minutes. Gently shake the bucket to remove the loaf, and turn it out onto a rack to cool.

Multigrain Honey Bread
PREP: 10 MINUTES / MAKES 1 LOAF

Ingredients

12 slice bread (1½ pounds)

1⅛ cups lukewarm milk

2¼ tablespoons unsalted butter, melted

3 tablespoons sugar

1½ teaspoons table salt

⅓ cup wheat bran

1½ tablespoons honey

1⅛ cups multigrain flour

2 cups white bread flour

1⅛ cups lukewarm water

2 tablespoons unsalted butter, melted

Directions
1. **Preparing the Ingredients**
   Choose the size of bread to prepare. Measure and add the ingredients to the pan in the order as indicated in the ingredient listing. Insert the bread pan in the Cuisinart Bread Machine.
2. **Select the Bake cycle**
   Close, Press the "Start" button. Select the White / Basic setting, then select the dough size and crust color. Press start to start the cycle.
   When this is done, and the bread is baked, remove the pan from the machine. Let stand a few minutes.
   Remove the bread from the skillet and leave it on a wire rack to cool for at least 10 minutes.
   Slice and serve.

Classic Dark Bread
PREP: 10 MINUTES / MAKES 1 LOAF

Ingredients
12 slice bread (1½ pounds)
1 cup lukewarm water
1½ tablespoons unsalted butter, melted
⅓ cup molasses
⅓ teaspoon table salt
¾ cup rye flour
2 cups white bread flour
2¼ cups whole-wheat bread flour
1½ tablespoons unsweetened cocoa powder
Pinch ground nutmeg
1⅔ teaspoons bread machine yeast

Directions
1. **Preparing the Ingredients.**
   Choose the size of bread to prepare. Measure and add the ingredients to the pan in the order as indicated in the ingredient listing. Insert the bread pan in the Cuisinart Bread Machine.

2. **Select the Bake cycle**
   Close, Press the "Start" button. Select the White / Basic setting, then select the dough size and crust color. Press start to start the cycle.
   When this is done, and the bread is baked, remove the pan from the machine. Let stand a few minutes.
   Remove the bread from the skillet and leave it on a wire rack to cool for at least 10 minutes. Slice and serve.

Classic Corn Bread
PREP: 10 MINUTES / MAKES 1 LOAF

Ingredients
12 slice bread (1½ pounds)
1 cup lukewarm buttermilk
¼ cup unsalted butter, melted
2 eggs, at room temperature
¼ cup sugar
1 teaspoon table salt
1⅓ cups all-purpose flour
1 cup cornmeal
1 tablespoon baking powder

Directions
1. **Preparing the Ingredients.**
   Choose the size of bread to prepare. Measure and add the ingredients to the pan in the order as indicated in the ingredient listing. Insert the bread pan in the Cuisinart Bread Machine.
2. **Select the Bake cycle**
   Close, Press the "Start" button. Select the White / Basic setting, then select the dough size, select light or medium crust. Press start to start the cycle.
   When this is done, and the bread is baked, remove the pan from the machine. Let stand a few minutes.
   Remove the bread from the skillet and leave it on a wire rack to cool for at least 10 minutes. Slice and serve.

Traditional Italian Bread
PREP: 10 MINUTES /MAKES 1 LOAF

Ingredients

12 slice bread (1½ pounds)
1 cup water, at 80°F to 90°F
1½ tablespoons olive oil
1½ tablespoons sugar
1⅛ teaspoons salt
3 cups white bread flour
2⅔ cups white bread flour
1½ teaspoons bread machine or instant yeast

Directions

1. **Preparing the Ingredients.**
   Place the ingredients in your bread maker as recommended by the manufacturer

2. **Select the Bake cycle**
   Close, Press the "Start" button. Select the White / Basic setting, then select the dough size, select light or medium crust. Press start to start the cycle.
   When this is done, and the bread is baked, remove the pan from the machine. Let stand a few minutes.
   Remove the bread from the skillet and leave it on a wire rack to cool for at least 10 minutes. Slice and serve.

Basic Seed Bread
PREP: 10 MINUTES /MAKES 1 LOAF

Ingredients

12 slice bread (1½ pounds)
1⅛ cups lukewarm water
1½ tablespoons unsalted butter, melted
1½ tablespoons sugar
1⅛ teaspoons table salt
2½ cups white bread flour
¾ cup ground chia seeds
2 tablespoons sesame seeds
1½ teaspoons bread machine yeast

Directions

1. **Preparing the Ingredients.**
   Choose the size of bread to prepare. Measure and add the ingredients to the pan in the order as indicated in the ingredient listing. Insert the bread pan in the Cuisinart Bread Machine.
2. **Select the Bake cycle**
   Close, Press the "Start" button. Select the White / Basic setting, then select the dough size, select light or medium crust. Press start to start the cycle.
   When this is done, and the bread is baked, remove the pan from the machine. Let stand a few minutes.
   Remove the bread from the skillet and leave it on a wire rack to cool for at least 10 minutes. Slice and serve.

Double-Chocolate Zucchini Bread
PREP: 10 MINUTES / MAKES 1 LOAF

Ingredients

225 grams grated zucchini
125 grams All-Purpose Flour Blend
50 grams all-natural unsweetened cocoa powder (not Dutch-process)
1 teaspoon xanthan gum
¾ teaspoon baking soda
¼ teaspoon baking powder
¼ teaspoon salt
½ teaspoon ground espresso
135 grams chocolate chips or nondairy alternative
100 grams cane sugar or granulated sugar
2 large eggs
¼ cup avocado oil or canola oil
60 grams vanilla Greek yogurt or nondairy alternative
1 teaspoon vanilla extract

Directions
1. **Preparing the Ingredients.**
   Measure and add the ingredients to the pan in the order mentioned above. Insert the bread pan in the Cuisinart Bread Machine.
2. **Select the Bake cycle**
   Press the "Start" button. Select the White / Basic setting, then select the dough size, select light or medium crust. Press start to start the cycle.
   When this is done, and the bread is baked, remove the pan from the machine. Let stand a few minutes.
   Remove the bread from the skillet and leave it on a wire rack to cool for at least 15 minutes. Store leftovers in an airtight container at room temperature for up to 5 days, or freeze to enjoy a slice whenever you desire. Let each slice thaw naturally

Basic Bulgur Bread
PREP: 10 MINUTES / MAKES 1 LOAF

Ingredients

16 slice bread (2 pounds)
½ cup lukewarm water
½ cup bulgur wheat
1⅓ cups lukewarm milk
1⅓ tablespoons unsalted butter, melted
1⅓ tablespoons sugar
1 teaspoon table salt
4 cups bread flour
3 cups whole-wheat bread flour
2 teaspoons bread machine yeast

Directions
1. **Preparing the Ingredients.**
   Measure and add the ingredients to the pan in the order mentioned above. Insert the bread pan in the Cuisinart Bread Machine.
2. **Select the Bake cycle**
   Close, Press the "Start" button. Select the White / Basic setting, then select the dough size, select light or medium crust. Press start to start the cycle.
   When this is done, and the bread is baked, remove the pan from the machine. Let stand a few minutes.
   Remove the bread from the skillet and leave it on a wire rack to cool for at least 10 minutes. Slice and serve.

Oat Quinoa Bread
PREP: 10 MINUTES / MAKES 1 LOAF

Ingredients
12 slice bread (1½ pounds)
1 cup lukewarm milk
⅔ cup cooked quinoa, cooled
¼ cup unsalted butter, melted
1 tablespoon sugar
1 teaspoon table salt
1½ cups white bread flour
¼ cup quick oats
¾ cup whole-wheat flour
1½ teaspoons bread machine yeast

Directions
1. **Preparing the Ingredients.**
   Measure and add the ingredients to the pan in the order mentioned above. Insert the bread pan in the Cuisinart Bread Machine.
2. **Select the Bake cycle**
   Close, Press the "Start" button. Select the White / Basic setting, then select the dough size, select light or medium crust. Press start to start the cycle.
   When this is done, and the bread is baked, remove the pan from the machine. Let stand a few minutes.
   Remove the bread from the skillet and leave it on a wire rack to cool for at least 10 minutes. Slice and serve.

SOURDOUGH BREADS

Basic Honey Bread
PREP: 10 MINUTES / MAKES 1 LOAF

Ingredients
12 slice bread (1½ pounds)
1½ cups warm milk
¼ cup unsalted butter, melted
2 eggs, beaten
1 teaspoon apple cider vinegar
½ cup honey
1 teaspoon table salt
3 cups gluten-free flour(s) of your choice
1½ teaspoons xanthan gum
1¾ teaspoons bread machine yeast

Directions
1. **Preparing the Ingredients.**
   Choose the size of loaf of your preference and then measure the ingredients.
   Add all of the ingredients mentioned previously in the list, Close after placing the pan in the Cuisinart Bread Machine.

2. **Select the Bake cycle**
   Turn on the Cuisinart Bread Machine. Select the White/Basic or Gluten-Free (if your machine has this setting) setting, select the loaf size, and the crust color. Press start.
   When the cycle is finished, remove the pan from the Cuisinart Bread Machine and let it rest.
   Take the bread out, put in a wire rack to cool for at least 10 minutes, and slice.

Multigrain Sourdough Bread
PREP: 10 MINUTES / MAKES 1 LOAF

Ingredients
12 slice bread (1½ pounds)
⅔ cup water, at 80°F to 90°F
¾ cup Simple Sourdough Starter, fed, active, and at room temperature
2 tablespoons melted butter, cooled
2½ tablespoons sugar
¾ teaspoon salt
¾ cup multigrain cereal
2⅔ cups white bread flour
1½ teaspoons bread machine or instant yeast

Directions
1. **Preparing the Ingredients.**
   Choose the size of loaf of your preference and then measure the ingredients.
   Add all of the ingredients mentioned previously in the list, Close after placing the pan in the Cuisinart Bread Machine.

2. **Select the Bake cycle**
   Turn on the Cuisinart Bread Machine. Select the Wheat/Whole-Grain bread setting, select the loaf size, and the crust color. Press start. When the cycle is finished, remove the pan from the Cuisinart Bread Machine and let it rest.
   Take the bread out, put in a wire rack to cool for at least 10 minutes, and slice.

Onion Buttermilk Bread
PREP: 10 MINUTES / MAKES 1 LOAF

Ingredients

12 slice bread (1½ pounds)
1 cup lukewarm water
3 tablespoons unsalted butter, melted
¾ teaspoon apple cider vinegar
3 tablespoons dry buttermilk powder
3 medium eggs, beaten
3 tablespoons sugar
1 teaspoon table salt
⅓ cup potato flour
⅓ cup tapioca flour
1½ cups white rice flour
¾ tablespoon dill, chopped
3 tablespoons green onion, chopped
2⅔ teaspoons xanthan gum
1½ teaspoons bread machine yeast

Directions

1. **Preparing the Ingredients.**
   Choose the size of loaf of your preference and then measure the ingredients.
   Add all of the ingredients mentioned previously in the list, Close after placing the pan in the Cuisinart Bread Machine.

2. **Select the Bake cycle**
   Turn on the Cuisinart Bread Machine. Select White/Basic or Gluten-Free (if your machine has this setting) setting, select the loaf size, and the crust color. Press start.
   When the cycle is finished, remove the pan from the Cuisinart Bread Machine and let it rest.
   Take the bread out, put in a wire rack to cool for at least 10 minutes, and slice.

Faux Sourdough Bread
PREP: 10 MINUTES / MAKES 1 LOAF

Ingredients

12 slice bread (1½ pounds)
¾ cup plus 1 tablespoon water, at 80°F to 90°F
⅓ cup sour cream, at room temperature
2¼ tablespoons melted butter, cooled
1½ tablespoons apple cider vinegar
¾ tablespoon sugar
¾ teaspoon salt
3 cups white bread flour
1 teaspoon bread machine or instant yeast

Directions

1. **Preparing the Ingredients.**
   Choose the size of loaf of your preference and then measure the ingredients.
   Add all of the ingredients mentioned previously in the list, Close after placing the pan in the Cuisinart Bread Machine.

2. **Select the Bake cycle**
   Turn on the Cuisinart Bread Machine. Select the Wheat/Whole-Grain bread setting, select the loaf size, select medium crust color. Press start.
   When the cycle is finished, remove the pan from the Cuisinart Bread Machine and let it rest.
   Take the bread out, put in a wire rack to cool for at least 10 minutes, and slice.

Pecan Cranberry Bread
PREP: 10 MINUTES /MAKES 1 LOAF

Ingredients

12 slice bread (1½ pounds)
1⅛ cups lukewarm water
3 tablespoons canola oil
¾ tablespoon orange zest
¾ teaspoon apple cider vinegar
2 eggs, slightly beaten
2¼ tablespoons sugar
¾ teaspoon table salt
1½ cups white rice flour
½ cup nonfat dry milk powder
⅓ cup tapioca flour
⅓ cup potato starch
¼ cup corn starch
¾ tablespoon xanthan gum
1½ teaspoons bread machine yeast
½ cup dried cranberries
½ cup pecan pieces

Directions
1. **Preparing the Ingredients.**
   Choose the size of loaf of your preference and then measure the ingredients.
2. Add all of the ingredients mentioned previously in the list, Close after placing the pan in the Cuisinart Bread Machine.
   Select the Bake cycle
   Press the "Start" button. Select the Gluten Free or Fruit/Nut (if your machine has this setting) setting, then the loaf size, and finally the crust color. Start the cycle. (If you don't have either of the above settings, use Basic/White.).
   Add the ingredients, add the pecans and cranberries when the bread maker indicates.
   When the Bread maker finish the Cycle, remove the pan from the Cuisinart Bread Machine and let it rest.
   Take the bread out, put in a wire rack to cool for at least 10 minutes, and slice.

Sourdough Milk Bread
PREP: 10 MINUTES /MAKES 1 LOAF

Ingredients

12 slice bread (1½ pounds)
1½ cups Simple Sourdough Starter (here) or No-Yeast Sourdough Starter (here), fed, active, and at room temperature
⅓ cup milk, at 80°F to 90°F
3 tablespoons olive oil
1½ tablespoons honey
1 teaspoon salt
3 cups white bread flour
1 teaspoon bread machine or instant yeast

Directions
1. **Preparing the Ingredients.**
   Choose the size of loaf of your preference and then measure the ingredients.
   Add all of the ingredients mentioned previously in the list, Close after placing the pan in the Cuisinart Bread Machine.

2. **Select the Bake cycle**
   Turn on the Cuisinart Bread Machine. Select the White/Basic setting, select the loaf size, and the crust color. Press start.
   When the cycle is finished, remove the pan from the Cuisinart Bread Machine and let it rest.
   Take the bread out, put in a wire rack to cool for at least 10 minutes, and slice.

Cheese Potato Bread

PREP: 10 MINUTES / MAKES 1 LOAF

Ingredients

12 slice bread (1½ pounds)
1 cup lukewarm water
2¼ tablespoons vegetable oil
2 large eggs, beaten
⅓ cup dry skim milk powder
3 tablespoons sugar
¾ teaspoon apple cider vinegar
1⅛ teaspoons table salt
⅓ cup cornstarch
½ cup cottage cheese
3 tablespoons snipped chives
⅓ cup instant potato buds
⅓ cup potato starch
⅓ cup tapioca flour
1½ cups white rice flour
1½ teaspoons bread machine yeast

Directions

1. **Preparing the Ingredients.**
   Choose the size of loaf of your preference and then measure the ingredients.
   Add all of the ingredients mentioned previously in the list, Close after placing the pan in the Cuisinart Bread Machine.

2. **Select the Bake cycle**
   Turn on the Cuisinart Bread Machine. Select the White/ Basic or Gluten-Free (if your machine has this setting) setting, select the loaf size, and the crust color. Press start.
   When the cycle is finished, remove the pan from the Cuisinart Bread Machine and let it rest.
   Take the bread out, put in a wire rack to cool for at least 10 minutes, and slice.

Lemon Sourdough Bread

PREP: 10 MINUTES / MAKES 1 LOAF

Ingredients

12 slice bread (1½ pounds)
¾ cup Simple Sourdough Starter (here) or No-Yeast Sourdough Starter (here), fed, active, and at room temperature
¾ cup water, at 80°F to 90°F
1 egg, at room temperature
3 tablespoons butter, melted and cooled
⅓ cup honey
1½ teaspoons salt
2 teaspoons lemon zest
1½ teaspoons lime zest
⅓ cup wheat germ
3 cups white bread flour
1¾ teaspoons bread machine or instant yeast

Directions

1. **Preparing the Ingredients.**
   Choose the size of loaf of your preference and then measure the ingredients.
2. Add all of the ingredients mentioned previously in the list, Close after placing the pan in the Cuisinart Bread Machine
   Select the Bake cycle.
   Turn on the Cuisinart Bread Machine. Select the Whole-Wheat/Whole-Grain bread setting, select the loaf size, select light or medium crust. Press start.
   When the cycle is finished, remove the pan from the Cuisinart Bread Machine and let it rest.
   Take the bread out, put in a wire rack to cool for at least 10 minutes, and slice.

FRUIT BREADS

Cranberry & Golden Raisin Bread
PREP: 10 MINUTES / MAKES 14 SLICES

Ingredients
1⅓ cups water
4 Tbsp sliced butter
3 cups flour
1 cup old fashioned oatmeal
⅓ cup brown sugar
1 tsp salt
4 Tbsp dried cranberries
4 Tbsp golden raisins
2 tsp bread machine yeast

Directions
1. **Preparing the Ingredients**
   Add each ingredient except cranberries and golden raisins to the Cuisinart Bread Machine one by one, according to the manufacturer's instructions.
2. **Select the Bake cycle**
   Close, select the sweet or basic bread, medium crust setting on your bread machine and press start.
   Add the cranberries and golden raisins 5 to 10 minutes before the last kneading cycle ends.
   When the Cuisinart Bread Machine has finished baking, remove the bread and put it on a cooling rack.

Zucchini Bread
PREP: 10 MINUTES / MAKES 2 LOAVES

Ingredients
3 cups shredded zucchini (2 to 3 medium)
12/3 cups sugar
2/3 cup vegetable oil
2 teaspoons vanilla
4 eggs
3 cups all-purpose or whole wheat flour
2 teaspoons baking soda
1 teaspoon salt
1 teaspoon ground cinnamon
½ teaspoon baking powder
½ teaspoon ground cloves
½ cup chopped nuts
½ cup raisins, if desired

Directions
1. **Preparing the Ingredients.**
   Choose the size of loaf of your preference and then measure the ingredients.
   Add all of the ingredients mentioned previously in the list. Close after placing the pan in the Cuisinart Bread Machine.
2. **Select the Bake cycle**
   Turn on the Cuisinart Bread Machine. Select the White/Basic setting, select the loaf size, and the crust color. Press start.
   When the cycle is finished, remove the pan from the Cuisinart Bread Machine and let it rest.
   Take the bread out, put in a wire rack to cool for at least 2 hours before slicing. Wrap tightly and store at room temperature up to 4 days, or refrigerate up to 10 days.

Cinnamon Figs Bread
PREP: 10 MINUTES / MAKES 1 LOAF

Ingredients
16 slice bread (1½ pounds)
1⅛ cups lukewarm water
2¼ tablespoons unsalted butter, melted
3 tablespoons sugar
¾ teaspoon table salt
⅓ teaspoon cinnamon, ground
¾ teaspoon orange zest
Pinch ground nutmeg
1⅞ cups whole-wheat flour
1⅛ cups white bread flour
1½ teaspoons bread machine yeast
1 cup chopped plums or sliced figs

Directions
1. **Preparing the Ingredients.**
   Choose the size of loaf of your preference and then measure the ingredients.
   Add all of the ingredients mentioned previously in the list, except for the plums. Close after placing the pan in the Cuisinart Bread Machine.
2. **Select the Bake cycle**
   Turn on the Cuisinart Bread Machine. White/Basic or Fruit/Nut (if your machine has this setting) setting, select the loaf size, and the crust color. Press start.
   When the machine signals to add ingredients, add the plums. When the cycle is finished, remove the pan from the Cuisinart Bread Machine and let it rest.
   Take the bread out, put in a wire rack to cool for at least 10 minutes, and slice.

Robust Date Bread
PREP: 10 MINUTES / MAKES 1 LOAF

Ingredients
12 slice bread (1½ pounds)
¾ cup water, at 80°F to 90°F
½ cup milk, at 80°F
2 tablespoons melted butter, cooled
¼ cup honey
3 tablespoons molasses
1 tablespoon sugar
2 tablespoons skim milk powder
1 teaspoon salt
2¼ cups whole-wheat flour
1¼ cups white bread flour
1 tablespoon unsweetened cocoa powder
1½ teaspoons bread machine or instant yeast
¾ cup chopped dates

Directions
1. **Preparing the Ingredients.**
   Choose the size of loaf of your preference and then measure the ingredients.
   Add all of the ingredients mentioned previously in the list. Close after placing the pan in the Cuisinart Bread Machine
2. **Select the Bake cycle**
   Turn on the Cuisinart Bread Machine. Select the White/Basic setting, select the loaf size, and the crust color. Press start.
   When the cycle is finished, remove the pan from the Cuisinart Bread Machine and let it rest.
   Take the bread out, put in a wire rack to cool for at least 10 minutes before slicing.

Cranberry Honey Bread
PREP: 10 MINUTES / MAKES 1 LOAF

Ingredients
16 slice bread (2 pounds)
1¼ cups + 1 tablespoon lukewarm water
¼ cup unsalted butter, melted
3 tablespoons honey or molasses
4 cups white bread flour
½ cup cornmeal
2 teaspoons table salt
2½ teaspoons bread machine yeast
¾ cup cranberries, dried

Directions
1. **Preparing the Ingredients.**
Choose the size of loaf of your preference and then measure the ingredients.
Add all of the ingredients mentioned previously in the list. Close after placing the pan in the Cuisinart Bread Machine
2. **Select the Bake cycle**
Press the "Start" button. Select the White/Basic or Fruit/Nut (if your machine has this setting) setting, then the loaf size, and finally the crust color. Start the cycle.
When the machine signals to add ingredients, add the dried cranberries.
When the cycle is finished, remove the pan from the bread maker. Let rest for a few minutes.
Take the bread out and allow to cool on a wire rack for at least 10 minutes before slicing.

Apple Spice Bread
PREP: 10 MINUTES / MAKES 1 LOAF

Ingredients
16 slice bread (2 pounds)
1⅓ cup milk, at 80°F to 90°F
3⅓ tablespoons melted butter, cooled
2⅔ tablespoons sugar
2 teaspoons salt
1⅓ teaspoons ground cinnamon
Pinch ground cloves
4 cups white bread flour
2¼ teaspoons bread machine or active dry yeast
1⅓ cups finely diced peeled apple

Directions
1. **Preparing the Ingredients.**
Choose the size of loaf of your preference and then measure the ingredients.
Add all of the ingredients mentioned previously in the list, except for the apple. Close after placing the pan in the Cuisinart Bread Machine.

2. **Select the Bake cycle**
Turn on the Cuisinart Bread Machine. White/Basic or Fruit/Nut (if your machine has this setting) setting, select the loaf size, and the crust color. Press start.
When the machine signals to add ingredients, add the apple. When the cycle is finished, remove the pan from the Cuisinart Bread Machine and let it rest.
Take the bread out, put in a wire rack to cool for at least 10 minutes, and slice.

Poppy Seed–Lemon Bread
PREP: 10 MINUTES / MAKES 1 LOAF

Ingredients

1 cup sugar
¼ cup grated lemon peel
1 cup milk
¾ cup vegetable oil
2 tablespoons poppy seed
2 teaspoons baking powder
½ teaspoon salt
2 eggs, slightly beaten

Directions

1. **Preparing the Ingredients.**
   Choose the size of loaf of your preference and then measure the ingredients.
   Add all of the ingredients mentioned previously in the list. Close after placing the pan in the Cuisinart Bread Machine
2. **Select the Bake cycle**
   Turn on the Cuisinart Bread Machine. Select the White/Basic setting, select the loaf size, and the crust color. Press start. When the cycle is finished, remove the pan from the Cuisinart Bread Machine and let it rest.
   Take the bread out, put in a wire rack to cool completely, about 2 hours. Store at room temperature for 3 to 4 days, or store in refrigerator.

Ginger-Carrot-Nut Bread
PREP: 10 MINUTES / MAKES 1 LOAF

Ingredients

2 eggs
¾ cup packed brown sugar
1/3 cup vegetable oil
½ cup milk
1 teaspoon vanilla
2 cups all-purpose flour
2 teaspoons baking powder
1 teaspoon ground ginger
½ teaspoon salt
1 cup shredded carrots (2 medium)
½ cup chopped nuts

Directions

1. **Preparing the Ingredients.**
   Choose the size of loaf of your preference and then measure the ingredients.
   Add all of the ingredients mentioned previously in the list. Close after placing the pan in the Cuisinart Bread Machine

2. **Select the Bake cycle**
   Turn on the Cuisinart Bread Machine. Select the White/Basic setting, select the loaf size, and the crust color. Press start. When the cycle is finished, remove the pan from the Cuisinart Bread Machine and let it rest.
   Take the bread out, put in a wire rack to cool. Cool completely, about 10 minutes. Store at room temperature for 3 to 4 days, or store in refrigerator.

Orange Bread
PREP: 10 MINUTES /MAKES 1 LOAF

Ingredients
16 slice bread (2 pounds)
1¼ cups lukewarm milk
¼ cup orange juice
¼ cup sugar
1½ tablespoons unsalted butter, melted
1¼ teaspoons table salt
4 cups white bread flour
Zest of 1 orange
1¾ teaspoons bread machine yeast

Directions
1. **Preparing the Ingredients.**
Choose the size of loaf of your preference and then measure the ingredients.
Add all of the ingredients mentioned previously in the list. Close after placing the pan in the Cuisinart Bread Machine

2. **Select the Bake cycle**
Turn on the Cuisinart Bread Machine. Select the White/Basic setting, select the loaf size, and the crust color. Press start.
When the cycle is finished, remove the pan from the Cuisinart Bread Machine and let it rest.
Take the bread out, put in a wire rack to cool. Cool completely, about 10 minutes. Slice

Lemon-Lime Blueberry Bread
PREP: 10 MINUTES /MAKES 1 LOAF

Ingredients
12 slice bread (1½ pounds)
¾ cup plain yogurt, at room temperature
½ cup water, at 80°F to 90°F
3 tablespoons honey
1 tablespoon melted butter, cooled
1½ teaspoons salt
½ teaspoon lemon extract
1 teaspoon lime zest
1 cup dried blueberries
3 cups white bread flour
2¼ teaspoons bread machine or instant yeast

Directions
1. **Preparing the Ingredients.**
Choose the size of loaf of your preference and then measure the ingredients.
Add all of the ingredients mentioned previously in the list. Close after placing the pan in the Cuisinart Bread Machine
2. **Select the Bake cycle**
Turn on the Cuisinart Bread Machine. Select the White/Basic setting, select the loaf size, and the crust color. Press start.
When the cycle is finished, remove the pan from the Cuisinart Bread Machine and let it rest.
Take the bread out, put in a wire rack to cool. Cool completely, about 10 minutes. Slice

Honey Banana Bread
PREP: 10 MINUTES / MAKES 1 LOAF

Ingredients
- 12 slice bread (1½ pounds)
- ½ cup lukewarm milk
- 1 cup banana, mashed
- 1 egg, beaten
- 1½ tablespoons unsalted butter, melted
- 3 tablespoons honey
- 1 teaspoon pure vanilla extract
- ½ teaspoon table salt
- 1 cup whole-wheat flour
- 1¼ cups white bread flour
- 1½ teaspoons bread machine yeast

Directions
1. **Preparing the Ingredients.**
   Choose the size of loaf of your preference and then measure the ingredients.
   Add all of the ingredients mentioned previously in the list. Close after placing the pan in the Cuisinart Bread Machine
2. **Select the Bake cycle**
   Press the "Start" button. Select the Sweet setting, then the loaf size, and finally the crust color. Start the cycle.
   When the cycle is finished remove the pan from the machine.
   Take the bread out and allow to cool on a wire rack for at least 10 minutes before slicing.

Banana Whole-Wheat Bread
PREP: 10 MINUTES / MAKES 1 LOAF

Ingredients
- 12 slice bread (1½ pounds)
- ½ cup milk, at 80°F to 90°F
- 1 cup mashed banana
- 1 egg, at room temperature
- 1½ tablespoons melted butter, cooled
- 3 tablespoons honey
- 1 teaspoon pure vanilla extract
- ½ teaspoon salt
- 1 cup whole-wheat flour
- 1¼ cups white bread flour
- 1½ teaspoons bread machine or instant yeast

Directions
1. **Preparing the Ingredients.** Choose the size of loaf of your preference and then measure the ingredients.
   Add all of the ingredients mentioned previously in the list. Close after placing the pan in the Cuisinart Bread Machine
2. **Select the Bake cycle.** Turn on the Cuisinart Bread Machine. Select the Sweet bread setting, select the loaf size, and the crust color. Press start. When the cycle is finished, remove the pan from the Cuisinart Bread Machine and let it rest. Shake the bucket to remove the loaf, and turn it out onto a rack to cool.

Oatmeal-Streusel Bread
PREP: 10 MINUTES / MAKES 1 LOAF

Ingredients
Streusel
¼ cup packed brown sugar
¼ cup chopped walnuts, toasted
2 teaspoons ground cinnamon

Bread
1 cup all-purpose flour
½ cup whole wheat flour
½ cup old-fashioned oats
2 tablespoons ground flaxseed or flaxseed meal
1 teaspoon baking powder
½ teaspoon salt
¼ teaspoon baking soda
¾ cup packed brown sugar
2/3 cup vegetable oil
2 eggs
¼ cup sour cream
2 teaspoons vanilla
½ cup milk

Icing
¾ to 1 cup powdered sugar
1 tablespoon milk
2 teaspoons light corn syrup

Directions
1. **Preparing the Ingredients.**
   Choose the size of loaf of your preference and then measure the ingredients.
   Add all of the ingredients mentioned previously in the list. Close after placing the pan in the Cuisinart Bread Machine
2. **Select the Bake cycle.**
   Turn on the Cuisinart Bread Machine. Select the White/Basic setting, select the loaf size, and the crust color. Press start.
   When the cycle is finished, remove the pan from the Cuisinart Bread Machine and let it rest.
   Take the bread out, put in a wire rack to Cool completely, about 2 hours.
   In small bowl, beat all icing ingredients, adding enough of the powdered sugar for desired drizzling consistency. Drizzle icing over bread. Let stand until set. Store at room temperature for 3 to 4 days, or store in refrigerator. To toast walnuts, bake in ungreased shallow pan at 350°F for 7 to 11 minutes, stirring occasionally, until light brown.

Garlic Olive Bread
PREP: 10 MINUTES / MAKES 1 LOAF

Ingredients
12 slice bread (1½ pounds)
1 cup lukewarm milk
1½ tablespoons unsalted butter, melted
1 teaspoon garlic, minced
1½ tablespoons sugar
1 teaspoon table salt
3 cups white bread flour
1 teaspoon bread machine yeast
⅓ cup black olives, chopped
16 slice bread (2 pounds)
1⅓ cups lukewarm milk
2 tablespoons unsalted butter, melted
1⅓ teaspoons garlic, minced
2 tablespoons sugar
1⅓ teaspoons table salt
4 cups white bread flour
1½ teaspoons bread machine yeast
½ cup black olives, chopped

Directions
1. **Preparing the Ingredients**
   Choose the size of loaf of your preference and then measure the ingredients.
   Add all of the ingredients mentioned previously in the list, except for the olives. Close after placing the pan in the Cuisinart Bread Machine.
2. **Select the Bake**
   Turn on the Cuisinart Bread Machine. White/Basic or Fruit/Nut (if your machine has this setting) setting, select the loaf size, and the crust color. Press start.
   When the machine signals to add ingredients, add the olives. When the cycle is finished, remove the pan from the Cuisinart Bread Machine and let it rest.
   Take the bread out, put in a wire rack to cool for at least 10 minutes, and slice.

Brown Bread with Raisins
PREP: 10 MINUTES / MAKES 1 LOAF

Ingredients
32 slices
1 cup all-purpose flour
1 cup whole wheat flour
1 cup whole-grain cornmeal
1 cup raisins
2 cups buttermilk
¾ cup molasses
2 teaspoons baking soda
1 teaspoon salt

Directions
1. **Preparing the Ingredients.**
   Choose the size of loaf of your preference and then measure the ingredients.
   Add all of the ingredients mentioned previously in the list. Close after placing the pan in the Cuisinart Bread Machine.
2. **Select the Bake cycle**
   Turn on the Cuisinart Bread Machine. Select the White/Basic setting, select the loaf size, and the crust color. Press start.
   When the cycle is finished, remove the pan from the Cuisinart Bread Machine and let it rest.
   Take the bread out, put in a wire rack to Cool completely, about 30 minutes.

Cinnamon Pumpkin Bread
PREP: 10 MINUTES / MAKES 1 LOAF

Ingredients
16 slice bread (2 pounds)
2 cups pumpkin puree
4 eggs, slightly beaten
½ cup unsalted butter, melted
1¼ cups sugar
½ teaspoon table salt
4 cups white bread flour
1 teaspoon cinnamon, ground
¾ teaspoon baking soda
½ teaspoon nutmeg, ground
½ teaspoon ginger, ground
Pinch ground cloves
2 teaspoons baking powder

Directions
1. **Preparing the Ingredients.**
   Choose the size of loaf of your preference and then measure the ingredients.
   Add all of the ingredients mentioned previously in the list. Close after placing the pan in the Cuisinart Bread Machine.

2. **Select the Bake cycle**
   Turn on the Cuisinart Bread Machine. Select the Quick/Rapid setting, select the loaf size, and the crust color. Press start.
   When the cycle is finished, remove the pan from the Cuisinart Bread Machine and let it rest.
   Take the bread out, put in a wire rack to Cool completely, about 30 minutes. Slice

Plum Orange Bread
PREP: 10 MINUTES / MAKES 1 LOAF

Ingredients
12 slice bread (1½ pounds)
1⅛ cup water, at 80°F to 90°F
2¼ tablespoons melted butter, cooled
3 tablespoons sugar
¾ teaspoon salt
¾ teaspoon orange zest
⅓ teaspoon ground cinnamon
Pinch ground nutmeg
1¾ cups plus 2 tablespoons whole-wheat flour
1⅛ cups white bread flour
1½ teaspoons bread machine or instant yeast
1 cup chopped fresh plums

Directions
1. **Preparing the Ingredients.**
   Choose the size of loaf of your preference and then measure the ingredients.
   Add all of the ingredients mentioned previously in the list, except for the plums. Close after placing the pan in the Cuisinart Bread Machine.
2. **Select the Bake cycle**
   Turn on the Cuisinart Bread Machine. White/Basic or Fruit/Nut (if your machine has this setting) setting, select the loaf size, and the crust color. Press start.
   When the machine signals to add ingredients, add the plums. When the cycle is finished, remove the pan from the Cuisinart Bread Machine and let it rest.
   Take the bread out, put in a wire rack to cool for at least 10 minutes, and slice.

Blueberries 'n Orange Bread
PREP: 10 MINUTES / MAKES 1 LOAF

Ingredients
18 slices bread
3 cups Original Bisquick mix
½ cup granulated sugar
1 tablespoon grated orange peel
½ cup milk
3 tablespoons vegetable oil
2 eggs
1 cup fresh or frozen (rinsed and drained) blueberries glaze
½ cup powdered sugar
3 to 4 teaspoons orange juice
Additional grated orange peel, if desired

Directions
1. **Preparing the Ingredients.**
   Choose the size of loaf of your preference and then measure the ingredients.
   Add all of the ingredients mentioned previously in the list. Close after placing the pan in the Cuisinart Bread Machine.
2. **Select the Bake cycle**
   Set the machine for Basic/White bread, select light or medium crust, and press Start. When the bread is done, remove the bucket from the machine. Let the loaf cool for 5 minutes.
   Gently shake the bucket to remove the loaf, and turn it out onto a rack to cool. Cool completely, about 45 minutes.
   In small bowl, mix powdered sugar and orange juice until smooth and thin enough to drizzle. Drizzle glaze over bread; sprinkle with additional orange peel.

Peaches and Cream Bread
PREP: 10 MINUTES / MAKES 1 LOAF

Ingredients
12 slice bread (1½ pounds)
¾ cup canned peaches, drained and chopped
⅓ cup heavy whipping cream, at 80°F to 90°F
1 egg, at room temperature
1 tablespoon melted butter, cooled
2¼ tablespoons sugar
1⅛ teaspoons salt
⅓ teaspoon ground cinnamon
⅛ teaspoon ground nutmeg
⅓ cup whole-wheat flour
2⅔ cups white bread flour
1⅛ teaspoons bread machine or instant yeast

Directions
1. **Preparing the Ingredients.**
   Choose the size of loaf of your preference and then measure the ingredients.
   Add all of the ingredients mentioned previously in the list. Close after placing the pan in the Cuisinart Bread Machine.
2. **Select the Bake cycle**
   Turn on the Cuisinart Bread Machine. Select the White/Basic setting, select the loaf size, and the crust color. Press start. When the cycle is finished, remove the pan from the Cuisinart Bread Machine and let it rest.
   Take the bread out, put in a wire rack to Cool completely, about 10 minutes.

Gluten-Free Glazed Lemon-Pecan Bread
PREP: 10 MINUTES /MAKES 1 LOAF

Ingredients
12 slice bread (1½ pounds)
½ cup white rice flour
½ cup tapioca flour
½ cup potato starch
¼ cup sweet white sorghum flour
¼ cup garbanzo and fava flour
1 teaspoon xanthan gum
1 teaspoon gluten-free baking powder
1 teaspoon baking soda
½ teaspoon salt
2 eggs
½ cup sunflower or canola oil or melted ghee
¼ cup almond milk, soymilk or regular milk
½ teaspoon cider vinegar
1 tablespoon grated lemon peel
¼ cup fresh lemon juice
2/3 cup granulated sugar
½ cup chopped pecans
glaze
2 tablespoons fresh lemon juice
1 cup gluten-free powdered sugar

Directions
1. **Preparing the Ingredients.** Choose the size of loaf of your preference and then measure the ingredients. Add all of the ingredients mentioned previously in the list. Close after placing the pan in the Cuisinart Bread Machine.
2. **Select the Bake cycle.** Turn on the Cuisinart Bread Machine. Select the White/Basic setting, select the loaf size, and the crust color. Press start. When the cycle is finished, remove the pan from the Cuisinart Bread Machine and let it rest. Take the bread out, put in a wire rack to Cool about 10 minutes.
In small bowl, stir all glaze ingredients until smooth. With fork, poke holes in top of loaf; drizzle glaze over loaf. Serve warm.

Fresh Blueberry Bread
PREP: 10 MINUTES /MAKES 1 LOAF

Ingredients
12 to 16 slices (1½ to 2 pounds)
1 cup plain Greek yogurt, at room temperature
½ cup milk, at room temperature
3 tablespoons butter, at room temperature
2 eggs, at room temperature
½ cup sugar
¼ cup light brown sugar
1 teaspoon pure vanilla extract
½ teaspoon lemon zest
2 cups all-purpose flour
1 tablespoon baking powder
¾ teaspoon salt
¼ teaspoon ground nutmeg
1 cup blueberries

Directions
1. **Preparing the Ingredients.** Place the yogurt, milk, butter, eggs, sugar, brown sugar, vanilla, and zest in your bread machine.
2. **Select the Bake cycle.** Set the machine for Quick/Rapid bread and press Start. While the wet ingredients are mixing, stir together the flour, baking powder, salt, and nutmeg in a medium bowl. After the first fast mixing is done, add the dry ingredients. When the second mixing cycle is complete, stir in the blueberries. When the bread is done, remove the bucket from the machine. Let the loaf cool for 5 minutes. Gently shake the bucket to remove the loaf, and turn it out onto a rack to cool.

Gluten-Free Best-Ever Banana Bread

PREP: 10 MINUTES / MAKES 1 LOAF

Ingredients

16 slices bread	1 teaspoon baking soda
½ cup tapioca flour	1 teaspoon salt
½ cup white rice flour	1 teaspoon ground cinnamon
½ cup potato starch	¾ cup packed brown sugar
¼ cup garbanzo and fava flour	1 cup mashed very ripe bananas (2 medium)
¼ cup sweet white sorghum flour	½ cup ghee (measured melted)
1 teaspoon xanthan gum	¼ cup almond milk, soymilk or regular milk
½ teaspoon guar gum	1 teaspoon gluten-free vanilla
1 teaspoon gluten-free baking powder	2 eggs

Directions

1. **Preparing the Ingredients.**
   Choose the size of loaf of your preference and then measure the ingredients. Add all of the ingredients mentioned previously in the list. Close after placing the pan in the Cuisinart Bread Machine.
2. **Select the Bake cycle**
   Turn on the Cuisinart Bread Machine. Select the White/Basic setting, select the loaf size, and the crust color. Press start. When the cycle is finished, remove the pan from the Cuisinart Bread Machine and let it rest. Take the bread out, put in a wire rack to Cool about 1 hour.

SPICE AND NUT BREAD

Cardamom Honey Bread
PREP: 10 MINUTES / MAKES 1 LOAF

Ingredients
16 slices bread (2 pounds)
1⅛ cups lukewarm milk
1 egg, at room temperature
2 teaspoons unsalted butter, melted
¼ cup honey
1⅓ teaspoons table salt
4 cups white bread flour
1⅓ teaspoons ground cardamom
1⅔ teaspoons bread machine yeast

Directions
1. **Preparing the Ingredients.**
   Choose the size of loaf of your preference and then measure the ingredients.
   Add all of the ingredients mentioned previously in the list.
   Close after placing the pan in the Cuisinart Bread Machine.

2. **Select the Bake cycle**
   Turn on the Cuisinart Bread Machine. Select the White/Basic setting, select the loaf size, and the crust color. Press start.
   When the cycle is finished, remove the pan from the Cuisinart Bread Machine and let it rest.
   Take the bread out, put in a wire rack to Cool about 10 minutes. Slice

Cracked Black Pepper Bread
PREP: 10 MINUTES / MAKES 1 LOAF

Ingredients
12 slice bread (1½ pounds)
1⅛ cups water, at 80°F to 90°F
1½ tablespoons melted butter, cooled
1½ tablespoons sugar
1 teaspoon salt
3 tablespoons skim milk powder
1½ tablespoons minced chives
¾ teaspoon garlic powder
¾ teaspoon freshly cracked black pepper
3 cups white bread flour
1¼ teaspoons bread machine or instant yeast

Directions
1. **Preparing the Ingredients.**
   Choose the size of loaf of your preference and then measure the ingredients.
   Add all of the ingredients mentioned previously in the list.
   Close after placing the pan in the Cuisinart Bread Machine.
2. **Select the Bake cycle**
   Turn on the Cuisinart Bread Machine. Select the White/Basic setting, select the loaf size, and the crust color. Press start.
   When the cycle is finished, remove the pan from the Cuisinart Bread Machine and let it rest.
   Take the bread out, put in a wire rack to Cool about 10 minutes. Slice

Pistachio Cherry Bread
PREP: 10 MINUTES / MAKES 1 LOAF

Ingredients
16 slices bread (2 pounds)
1⅛ cups lukewarm water
1 egg, at room temperature
¼ cup butter, softened
¼ cup packed dark brown sugar
1½ teaspoons table salt
3¾ cups white bread flour
½ teaspoon ground nutmeg
Dash allspice
2 teaspoons bread machine yeast
1 cup dried cherries
½ cup unsalted pistachios, chopped

Directions
1. **Preparing the Ingredients.**
   Choose the size of loaf of your preference and then measure the ingredients.
   Add all of the ingredients mentioned previously in the list, except the pistachios and cherries.
   Close after placing the pan in the Cuisinart Bread Machine.
2. **Select the Bake cycle**
   Press the "Start" button. Select the White/Basic or Fruit/Nut (if your machine has this setting) setting, then the loaf size, and finally the crust color. Press start.
   When the machine signals to add ingredients, add the pistachios and cherries.
   When the cycle is finished, remove the pan from the bread maker. Let rest for a few minutes.
   Take the bread out and allow to cool on a wire rack for at least 10 minutes before slicing.

Herb and Garlic Cream Cheese Bread
PREP: 10 MINUTES / MAKES 1 LOAF

Ingredients
12 slices bread (1½ pounds)
½ cup water, at 80°F to 90°F
½ cup herb and garlic cream cheese, at room temperature
1 egg, at room temperature
2 tablespoons melted butter, cooled
3 tablespoons sugar
1 teaspoon salt
3 cups white bread flour
1½ teaspoons bread machine or instant yeast

Directions
1. **Preparing the Ingredients.**
   Choose the size of loaf of your preference and then measure the ingredients.
   Add all of the ingredients mentioned previously in the list.
   Close after placing the pan in the Cuisinart Bread Machine.
2. **Select the Bake cycle**
   Turn on the Cuisinart Bread Machine. Select the White/Basic setting, select the loaf size, and the crust color. Press start.
   When the cycle is finished, remove the pan from the Cuisinart Bread Machine and let it rest.
   Take the bread out, put in a wire rack to Cool about 10 minutes. Slice

Mix Seed Raisin Bread
PREP: 10 MINUTES / MAKES 1 LOAF

Ingredients
16 slices bread (2 pounds)
1½ cups lukewarm milk
2 tablespoons unsalted butter, melted
2 tablespoons honey
1 teaspoon table salt
2½ cups white bread flour
¼ cup flaxseed
¼ cup sesame seeds
1½ cups whole-wheat flour
2¼ teaspoons bread machine yeast
½ cup raisins

Directions
1. **Preparing the Ingredients.**
   Choose the size of loaf of your preference and then measure the ingredients.
   Add all of the ingredients mentioned previously in the list.
   Close after placing the pan in the Cuisinart Bread Machine.
2. **Select the Bake cycle**
   Turn on the Cuisinart Bread Machine. Select the White/Basic setting, select the loaf size, and the crust color. Press start.
   When the cycle is finished, remove the pan from the Cuisinart Bread Machine and let it rest.
   Take the bread out, put in a wire rack to Cool about 10 minutes. Slice

Grain, Seed And Nut Bread
PREP: 10 MINUTES / MAKES 1 LOAF

Ingredients
¼ cup water
1 egg
3 Tbsp honey
1½ tsp butter, softened
3¼ cups bread flour
1 cup milk
1 tsp salt
¼ tsp baking soda
1 tsp ground cinnamon
2½ tsp active dry yeast
¾ cup dried cranberries
½ cup chopped walnuts
1 Tbsp white vinegar
½ tsp sugar

Directions
1. **Preparing the Ingredients.**
   Choose the size of loaf of your preference and then measure the ingredients.
   Add all of the ingredients mentioned previously in the list.
   Close after placing the pan in the Cuisinart Bread Machine.
2. **Select the Bake cycle**
   Turn on the Cuisinart Bread Machine. Select the White/Basic setting, select the loaf size, and the crust color. Press start.
   When the cycle is finished, remove the pan from the Cuisinart Bread Machine and let it rest.
   Take the bread out, put in a wire rack to Cool about 10 minutes. Slice

Honey-Spice Egg Bread
PREP: 10 MINUTES / MAKES 1 LOAF

Ingredients
12 slices bread (1½ pounds)
1 cup milk, at 80°F to 90°F
2 eggs, at room temperature
1½ tablespoons melted butter, cooled
2 tablespoons honey
1 teaspoon salt
1 teaspoon ground cinnamon
½ teaspoon ground cardamom
½ teaspoon ground nutmeg
3 cups white bread flour
2 teaspoons bread machine or instant yeast

Directions
1. **Preparing the Ingredients.**
   Choose the size of loaf of your preference and then measure the ingredients.
   Add all of the ingredients mentioned previously in the list.
   Close after placing the pan in the Cuisinart Bread Machine.
2. **Select the Bake cycle**
   Turn on the Cuisinart Bread Machine. Select the White/Basic setting, select the loaf size, and the crust color. Press start.
   When the cycle is finished, remove the pan from the Cuisinart Bread Machine and let it rest.
   Take the bread out, put in a wire rack to Cool about 10 minutes. Slice

Anise Honey Bread
PREP: 10 MINUTES / MAKES 1 LOAF

Ingredients
16 slices bread (2 pounds)
1 cup + 1 tablespoon lukewarm water
1 egg, at room temperature
⅓ cup butter, melted and cooled
⅓ cup honey
⅔ teaspoon table salt
4 cups white bread flour
1⅓ teaspoons anise seed
1⅓ teaspoons lemon zest
2½ teaspoons bread machine yeast

Directions
1. **Preparing the Ingredients.**
   Choose the size of loaf of your preference and then measure the ingredients.
   Add all of the ingredients mentioned previously in the list.
   Close after placing the pan in the Cuisinart Bread Machine.
2. **Select the Bake cycle**
   Turn on the Cuisinart Bread Machine. Select the White/Basic setting, select the loaf size, and the crust color. Press start.
   When the cycle is finished, remove the pan from the Cuisinart Bread Machine and let it rest.
   Take the bread out, put in a wire rack to Cool about 10 minutes. Slice

Basic Pecan Bread
PREP: 10 MINUTES /MAKES 1 LOAF

Ingredients
16 slices bread (2 pounds)
1⅓ cups lukewarm milk
2⅔ tablespoons unsalted butter, melted
1 egg, at room temperature
2⅔ tablespoons sugar
1⅓ teaspoons table salt
4 cups white bread flour
2 teaspoons bread machine yeast
1⅓ cups chopped pecans, toasted

Directions
1. **Preparing the Ingredients.**
   Choose the size of loaf of your preference and then measure the ingredients.
   Add all of the ingredients mentioned previously in the list, except the toasted pecans.
   Close after placing the pan in the Cuisinart Bread Machine.

2. **Select the Bake cycle**
   Select the White/Basic or Fruit/Nut (if your machine has this setting) setting, then the loaf size, and the crust color. Press start.
   When the machine signals to add ingredients, add the toasted pecans.
   When the cycle is finished, remove the pan from the Cuisinart Bread Machine and let it rest.
   Take the bread out, put in a wire rack to Cool about 10 minutes. Slice

Apple Walnut Bread
PREP: 10 MINUTES PLUS FERMENTING TIME /MAKES 1 LOAF

Ingredients
¾ cup unsweetened applesauce
4 cups apple juice
1 tsp salt
3 Tbsp butter
1 large egg
4 cups bread flour
¼ cup brown sugar, packed
1¼ tsp cinnamon
½ tsp baking soda
2 tsp active dry yeast
½ cup chopped walnuts
½ cup chopped dried cranberries

Directions
1. **Preparing the Ingredients**
   Add each ingredient to the Cuisinart Bread Machine in the order and at the temperature recommended by your bread machine manufacturer.
2. **Select the Bake cycle**
   Close, select the basic bread, medium crust setting on your bread machine, and press start.
   When the Cuisinart Bread Machine has finished baking, remove the bread and put it on a cooling rack.

Simple Garlic Bread
PREP: 10 MINUTES /MAKES 1 LOAF

Ingredients

12 slices bread (1½ pounds)
1 cup milk, at 70°F to 80°F
1½ tablespoons melted butter, cooled
1 tablespoon sugar
1½ teaspoons salt
2 teaspoons garlic powder
2 teaspoons chopped fresh parsley
3 cups white bread flour
1¾ teaspoons bread machine or instant yeast

Directions
1. **Preparing the Ingredients.**
   Choose the size of loaf of your preference and then measure the ingredients.
   Add all of the ingredients mentioned previously in the list.
   Close after placing the pan in the Cuisinart Bread Machine.
2. **Select the Bake cycle**
   Turn on the Cuisinart Bread Machine. Select the White/Basic setting, select the loaf size, and the crust color. Press start.
   When the cycle is finished, remove the pan from the Cuisinart Bread Machine and let it rest.
   Take the bread out, put in a wire rack to Cool about 10 minutes. Slice

Herbed Pesto Bread
PREP: 10 MINUTES /MAKES 1 LOAF

Ingredients

12 slices bread (1½ pounds)
1 cup water, at 80°F to 90°F
2¼ tablespoons melted butter, cooled
1½ teaspoons minced garlic
¾ tablespoon sugar
1 teaspoon salt
3 tablespoons chopped fresh parsley
1½ tablespoons chopped fresh basil
⅓ cup grated Parmesan cheese
3 cups white bread flour
1¼ teaspoons bread machine or active dry yeast

Directions
1. **Preparing the Ingredients.**
   Choose the size of loaf of your preference and then measure the ingredients.
   Add all of the ingredients mentioned previously in the list.
   Close after placing the pan in the Cuisinart Bread Machine.
2. **Select the Bake cycle**
   Turn on the Cuisinart Bread Machine. Select the White/Basic setting, select the loaf size, and the crust color. Press start.
   When the cycle is finished, remove the pan from the Cuisinart Bread Machine and let it rest.
   Take the bread out, put in a wire rack to Cool about 10 minutes. Slice

Caraway Rye Bread
PREP: 10 MINUTES / MAKES 1 LOAF

Ingredients

12 slice bread (1½ pounds)
1⅛ cups water, at 80°F to 90°F
1¾ tablespoons melted butter, cooled
3 tablespoons dark brown sugar
1½ tablespoons dark molasses
1⅛ teaspoons salt
1½ teaspoons caraway seed
¾ cup dark rye flour
2 cups white bread flour
1⅛ teaspoons bread machine or instant yeast

Directions
1. **Preparing the Ingredients.**
   Choose the size of loaf of your preference and then measure the ingredients.
   Add all of the ingredients mentioned previously in the list.
   Close after placing the pan in the Cuisinart Bread Machine.
2. **Select the Bake cycle**
   Turn on the Cuisinart Bread Machine. Select the White/Basic setting, select the loaf size, and the crust color. Press start.
   When the cycle is finished, remove the pan from the Cuisinart Bread Machine and let it rest.
   Take the bread out, put in a wire rack to Cool about 10 minutes. Slice

Anise Lemon Bread
PREP: 10 MINUTES / MAKES 1 LOAF

Ingredients

12 slice bread (1½ pounds)
¾ cup water, at 80°F to 90°F
1 egg, at room temperature
¼ cup butter, melted and cooled
¼ cup honey
½ teaspoon salt
1 teaspoon anise seed
1 teaspoon lemon zest
3 cups white bread flour
2 teaspoons bread machine or instant yeast

Directions
1. **Preparing the Ingredients.**
   Choose the size of loaf of your preference and then measure the ingredients.
   Add all of the ingredients mentioned previously in the list.
   Close after placing the pan in the Cuisinart Bread Machine.
2. **Select the Bake cycle**
   Turn on the Cuisinart Bread Machine. Select the White/Basic setting, select the loaf size, and the crust color. Press start.
   When the cycle is finished, remove the pan from the Cuisinart Bread Machine and let it rest.
   Take the bread out, put in a wire rack to Cool about 10 minutes. Slice

Fragrant Cardamom Bread
PREP: 10 MINUTES / MAKES 1 LOAF

Ingredients

12 slices bread (1½ pounds)
¾ cup milk, at 80°F to 90°F
1 egg, at room temperature
1½ teaspoons melted butter, cooled
3 tablespoons honey
1 teaspoon salt
1 teaspoon ground cardamom
3 cups white bread flour
1¼ teaspoons bread machine or instant yeast

Directions
1. **Preparing the Ingredients.**
   Choose the size of loaf of your preference and then measure the ingredients.
   Add all of the ingredients mentioned previously in the list.
   Close after placing the pan in the Cuisinart Bread Machine.
2. **Select the Bake cycle**
   Turn on the Cuisinart Bread Machine. Select the White/Basic setting, select the loaf size, and the crust color. Press start.
   When the cycle is finished, remove the pan from the Cuisinart Bread Machine and let it rest.
   Take the bread out, put in a wire rack to Cool about 10 minutes. Slice

Chocolate Mint Bread
PREP: 10 MINUTES / MAKES 1 LOAF

Ingredients

12 slices bread (1½ pounds)
1 cup milk, at 80°F to 90°F
⅛ teaspoon mint extract
1½ tablespoons butter, melted and cooled
¼ cup sugar
1 teaspoon salt
1½ tablespoons unsweetened cocoa powder
3 cups white bread flour
1¾ teaspoons bread machine or instant yeast
½ cup semisweet chocolate chips

Directions
1. **Preparing the Ingredients.**
   Choose the size of loaf of your preference and then measure the ingredients.
   Add all of the ingredients mentioned previously in the list.
   Close after placing the pan in the Cuisinart Bread Machine.
2. **Select the Bake cycle**
   Turn on the Cuisinart Bread Machine. Select the White/Basic setting, select the loaf size, and the crust color. Press start.
   When the cycle is finished, remove the pan from the Cuisinart Bread Machine and let it rest.
   Take the bread out, put in a wire rack to Cool about 5 minutes. Slice

Molasses Candied-Ginger Bread
PREP: 10 MINUTES /MAKES 1 LOAF

Ingredients

12 slices bread (1½ pounds)
1 cup milk, at 80°F to 90°F
1 egg, at room temperature
¼ cup dark molasses
3 tablespoons butter, melted and cooled
½ teaspoon salt
¼ cup chopped candied ginger
½ cup quick oats
3 cups white bread flour
2 teaspoons bread machine or instant yeast

Directions
1. **Preparing the Ingredients.**
   Choose the size of loaf of your preference and then measure the ingredients.
   Add all of the ingredients mentioned previously in the list.
   Close after placing the pan in the Cuisinart Bread Machine.

2. **Select the Bake cycle**
   Turn on the Cuisinart Bread Machine. Select the White/Basic setting, select the loaf size, and the crust color. Press start.
   When the cycle is finished, remove the pan from the Cuisinart Bread Machine and let it rest.
   Take the bread out, put in a wire rack to Cool about 5 minutes. Slice

Whole-Wheat Seed Bread
PREP: 10 MINUTES /MAKES 1 LOAF

Ingredients

12 slice bread (1½ pounds)
1⅛ cups water, at 80°F to 90°F
1½ tablespoons honey
1½ tablespoons melted butter, cooled
¾ teaspoon salt
2½ cups whole-wheat flour
¾ cup white bread flour
3 tablespoons raw sunflower seeds
1 tablespoon sesame seeds
1½ teaspoons bread machine or instant yeast

Directions
1. **Preparing the Ingredients.**
   Choose the size of loaf of your preference and then measure the ingredients.
   Add all of the ingredients mentioned previously in the list.
   Close after placing the pan in the Cuisinart Bread Machine.

2. **Select the Bake cycle**
   Turn on the Cuisinart Bread Machine. Select the Whole-Wheat/Whole-Grain bread, select the loaf size, and select light or medium crust. Press start.
   When the cycle is finished, remove the pan from the Cuisinart Bread Machine and let it rest.
   Take the bread out, put in a wire rack to Cool about 5 minutes. Slice

Multigrain Bread

PREP: 10 MINUTES / MAKES 1 LOAF

Ingredients
12 slice bread (1½ pounds)
1 cup plus 2 tablespoons water, at 80°F to 90°F
2 tablespoons melted butter, cooled
1½ tablespoons honey
1½ teaspoons salt
1 cup plus 2 tablespoons multigrain flour
2 cups white bread flour
1½ teaspoons bread machine or active dry yeast

Directions
1. **Preparing the Ingredients.**
   Choose the size of loaf of your preference and then measure the ingredients.
   Add all of the ingredients mentioned previously in the list.
   Close after placing the pan in the Cuisinart Bread Machine.
2. **Select the Bake cycle**
   Turn on the Cuisinart Bread Machine. Select the White/Basic setting, select the loaf size, and the crust color. Press start.
   When the cycle is finished, remove the pan from the Cuisinart Bread Machine and let it rest.
   Take the bread out, put in a wire rack to Cool about 5 minutes. Slice

Pecan Raisin Bread

PREP: 10 MINUTES PLUS FERMENTING TIME / MAKES 1 LOAF

Ingredients
1 cup plus 2 Tbsp water (70°F to 80°F)
8 tsp butter
1 egg
6 Tbsp sugar
¼ cup nonfat dry milk powder
1 tsp salt
4 cups bread flour
1 Tbsp active dry yeast
1 cup finely chopped pecans
1 cup raisins

Directions
1. **Preparing the Ingredients**
   Add each ingredient to the Cuisinart Bread Machine except the pecans and raisins in the order and at the temperature recommended by your bread machine manufacturer.
2. **Select the Bake cycle**
   Close, select the basic bread, medium crust setting on your bread machine, and press start.
   Just before the final kneading, add the pecans and raisins.
   When the Cuisinart Bread Machine has finished baking, remove the bread and put it on a cooling rack.

Toasted Pecan Bread
PREP: 10 MINUTES /MAKES 1 LOAF

Ingredients

12 slice bread (1½ pounds)
1 cup milk, at 70°F to 80°F
2 tablespoons melted butter, cooled
1 egg, at room temperature
2 tablespoons sugar
1 teaspoon salt
3 cups white bread flour
1½ teaspoons bread machine or instant yeast
1 cup chopped pecans, toasted

Directions
1. **Preparing the Ingredients.**
   Add each ingredient to the Cuisinart Bread Machine except the pecans and raisins in the order and at the temperature recommended by your bread machine manufacturer.
2. **Select the Bake cycle**
   Set the machine for Basic/White bread, select light or medium crust, and press Start.
   When the machine signals, add the pecans, or put them in a nut/raisin hopper and the machine will add them automatically
   When the cycle is finished, remove the pan from the Cuisinart Bread Machine and let it rest.
   Take the bread out, put in a wire rack to Cool about 5 minutes. Slice

Quinoa Oatmeal Bread
PREP: 10 MINUTES /MAKES 1 LOAF

Ingredients

⅓ cup uncooked quinoa
⅔ cup water (for cooking quinoa)
1 cup buttermilk
1 tsp salt
1 Tbsp sugar
1 Tbsp honey
4 Tbsp unsalted butter
½ cup quick-cooking oats
½ cup whole wheat flour
1½ cups bread flour

Directions
1. **Preparing the Ingredients**
   Add quinoa to a saucepan. Cover it with water. Bring to boil. Cook for 5 minutes, covered. Turn off and leave the quinoa covered for 10 minutes. Add each ingredient to the Cuisinart Bread Machine in the order and at the temperature recommended by your bread machine manufacturer.
2. **Select the Bake cycle**
   Close, select the whole grain, medium crust setting on your bread machine and press start. When the Cuisinart Bread Machine has finished baking, remove the bread and put it on a cooling rack.

Market Seed Bread
PREP: 10 MINUTES / MAKES 1 LOAF

Ingredients
12 slice bread (1½ pounds)
1 cup plus 2 tablespoons milk, at 80°F to 90°F
1½ tablespoons melted butter, cooled
1½ tablespoons honey
¾ teaspoon salt
3 tablespoons flaxseed
3 tablespoons sesame seeds
1½ tablespoons poppy seeds
1¼ cups whole-wheat flour
1¾ cups white bread flour
1¾ teaspoons bread machine or instant yeast

Directions
1. **Preparing the Ingredients.**
   Choose the size of loaf of your preference and then measure the ingredients.
   Add all of the ingredients mentioned previously in the list.
   Close after placing the pan in the Cuisinart Bread Machine.

2. **Select the Bake cycle**
   Turn on the Cuisinart Bread Machine. Select the White/Basic setting, select the loaf size, and the crust color. Press start.
   When the cycle is finished, remove the pan from the Cuisinart Bread Machine and let it rest.
   Take the bread out, put in a wire rack to Cool about 5 minutes. Slice

Pesto Nut Bread
PREP: 10 MINUTES / MAKES 14 SLICES

Ingredients
1 cup plus 2 Tbsp water
3 cups Gold Medal Better for Bread flour
2 Tbsp sugar
1 tsp salt
1¼ tsp bread machine or quick active dry yeast
For the pesto filling:
⅓ cup basil pesto
2 Tbsp Gold Medal Better for Bread flour
⅓ cup pine nuts

Directions
1. **Preparing the Ingredients**
   Add each ingredient to the Cuisinart Bread Machine in the order and at the temperature recommended by your bread machine manufacturer.
2. **Select the Bake cycle**
   Close, select the basic bread, medium crust setting on your bread machine, and press start.
   In a small bowl, combine pesto and 2 Tbsp of flour until well blended. Stir in the pine nuts. Add the filling 5 minutes before the last kneading cycle ends.
   When the Cuisinart Bread Machine has finished baking, remove the bread and put it on a cooling rack.

Cracked Wheat Bread
PREP: 10 MINUTES /MAKES 1 LOAF

Ingredients

12 slice bread (1½ pounds)
¼ cup cracked wheat
1¼ cups boiling water
¼ cup melted butter, cooled
3 tablespoons honey
1½ teaspoons salt
1 cup whole-wheat flour
2 cups white bread flour
2 teaspoons bread machine or instant yeast

Directions
1. **Preparing the Ingredients.**
   Place the cracked wheat and water in the bucket of your bread machine for 30 minutes or until the liquid is 80°F to 90°F.
   Place the remaining ingredients in your bread machine as recommended by the manufacturer.
2. **Select the Bake cycle**
   Turn on the Cuisinart Bread Machine. Select the White/Basic setting, select the loaf size, and the crust color. Press start.
   When the cycle is finished, remove the pan from the Cuisinart Bread Machine and let it rest.
   Take the bread out, put in a wire rack to Cool about 5 minutes. Slice

Double Coconut Bread
PREP: 10 MINUTES /MAKES 1 LOAF

Ingredients

12 slice bread (1½ pounds)
1 cup milk, at 80°F to 90°F
1 egg, at room temperature
1½ tablespoons melted butter, cooled
2 teaspoons pure coconut extract
2½ tablespoons sugar
¾ teaspoon salt
½ cup sweetened shredded coconut
3 cups white bread flour
1½ teaspoons bread machine or instant yeast

Directions
1. **Preparing the Ingredients.**
   Choose the size of loaf of your preference and then measure the ingredients.
   Add all of the ingredients mentioned previously in the list.
   Close after placing the pan in the Cuisinart Bread Machine.
2. **Select the Bake cycle**
   Set the machine for Sweet bread, select light or medium crust, and press Start.
   When the cycle is finished, remove the pan from the Cuisinart Bread Machine and let it rest.
   Take the bread out, put in a wire rack to Cool about 5 minutes. Slice

Seed Bread
PREP: 10 MINUTES / MAKES 1 LOAF

Ingredients
3 Tbsp flax seed
1 Tbsp sesame seeds
1 Tbsp poppy seeds
¾ cup water
1 Tbsp honey
1 Tbsp canola oil
½ tsp salt
1½ cups bread flour
5 Tbsp wholemeal flour
1¼ tsp dried active baking yeast

Directions
1. **Preparing the Ingredients**
   Add each ingredient to the Cuisinart Bread Machine in the order and at the temperature recommended by your bread machine manufacturer.
2. **Select the Bake cycle**
   Close, select the basic bread, medium crust setting on your bread machine, and press start.
   When the Cuisinart Bread Machine has finished baking, remove the bread and put it on a cooling rack.

Honeyed Bulgur Bread
PREP: 10 MINUTES / MAKES 1 LOAF

Ingredients
12 slice bread (1½ pounds)
¾ cup boiling water
3 tablespoons bulgur wheat
3 tablespoons quick oats
2 eggs, at room temperature
1½ tablespoons melted butter, cooled
2¼ tablespoons honey
1 teaspoon salt
2¼ cups white bread flour
1½ teaspoons bread machine or instant yeast

Directions
1. **Preparing the Ingredients.**
   Place the water, bulgur, and oats in the bucket of your bread machine for 30 minutes or until the liquid is 80°F to 90°F.
   Place the remaining ingredients in your bread machine as recommended by the manufacturer.
2. **Select the Bake cycle**
   Turn on the Cuisinart Bread Machine. Select the White/Basic setting, select the loaf size, and the crust color. Press start.
   When the cycle is finished, remove the pan from the Cuisinart Bread Machine and let it rest.
   Take the bread out, put in a wire rack to Cool about 5 minutes. Slice

Chia Seed Bread
PREP: 10 MINUTES /MAKES 14 SLICES

Ingredients
¼ cup chia seeds
¾ cup hot water
2⅜ cups water
¼ cup oil
½ lemon, zest and juice
1¾ cups white flour
1¾ cups whole wheat flour
2 tsp baking powder
1 tsp salt
1 Tbsp sugar
2½ tsp quick rise yeast

Directions
1. **Preparing the Ingredients**
   Add the chia seeds to a bowl, cover with hot water, mix well and let them stand until they are soaked and gelatinous, and don't feel warm to touch.
   Add each ingredient to the Cuisinart Bread Machine in the order and at the temperature recommended by your bread machine manufacturer.
2. **Select the Bake cycle**
   Close, select the basic bread, medium crust setting on your bread machine, and press start.
   When the mixing blade stops moving, open the machine and mix everything by hand with a spatula.
   When the Cuisinart Bread Machine has finished baking, remove the bread and put it on a cooling rack.

Flaxseed Honey Bread
PREP: 10 MINUTES /MAKES 1 LOAF

Ingredients
12 slices bread (1½ pounds)
1⅛ cups milk, at 80°F to 90°F
1½ tablespoons melted butter, cooled
1½ tablespoons honey
1 teaspoon salt
¼ cup flaxseed
3 cups white bread flour
1¼ teaspoons bread machine or instant yeast

Directions
1. **Preparing the Ingredients.**
   Choose the size of loaf of your preference and then measure the ingredients.
   Add all of the ingredients mentioned previously in the list.
   Close after placing the pan in the Cuisinart Bread Machine.
2. **Select the Bake cycle.**
   Turn on the Cuisinart Bread Machine. Select the White/Basic setting, select the loaf size, and the crust color. Press start.
   When the cycle is finished, remove the pan from the Cuisinart Bread Machine and let it rest.
   Take the bread out, put in a wire rack to Cool about 5 minutes. Slice

Chia Sesame Bread
PREP: 10 MINUTES / MAKES 1 LOAF

Ingredients
12 slice bread (1½ pounds)
1 cup plus 2 tablespoons water, at 80°F to 90°F
1½ tablespoons melted butter, cooled
1½ tablespoons sugar
1⅛ teaspoons salt
½ cup ground chia seeds
1½ tablespoons sesame seeds
2½ cups white bread flour
1½ teaspoons bread machine or instant yeast

Directions
1. **Preparing the Ingredients.**
   Choose the size of loaf of your preference and then measure the ingredients.
   Add all of the ingredients mentioned previously in the list.
   Close after placing the pan in the Cuisinart Bread Machine.
2. **Select the Bake cycle**
   Turn on the Cuisinart Bread Machine. Select the White/Basic setting, select the loaf size, and the crust color. Press start.
   When the cycle is finished, remove the pan from the Cuisinart Bread Machine and let it rest.
   Take the bread out, put in a wire rack to Cool about 5 minutes. Slice

Sesame French Bread
PREP: 10 MINUTES / MAKES 1 LOAF

Ingredients
⅞ cup water
1 Tbsp butter, softened
3 cups bread flour
2 tsp sugar
1 tsp salt
2 tsp yeast
2 Tbsp sesame seeds toasted

Directions
Preparing the Ingredients
Add each ingredient to the Cuisinart Bread Machine in the order and at the temperature recommended by your bread machine manufacturer.
Select the Bake cycle
Close, select the French bread, medium crust setting on your bread machine and press start.
When the Cuisinart Bread Machine has finished baking, remove the bread and put it on a cooling rack.

Quinoa Whole-Wheat Bread
PREP: 10 MINUTES /MAKES 1 LOAF

Ingredients
12 slice bread (1½ pounds)
1 cup milk, at 80°F to 90°F
⅔ cup cooked quinoa, cooled
¼ cup melted butter, cooled
1 tablespoon sugar
1 teaspoon salt
¼ cup quick oats
¾ cup whole-wheat flour
1½ cups white bread flour
1½ teaspoons bread machine or instant yeast

Directions
1. **Preparing the Ingredients.**
   Choose the size of loaf of your preference and then measure the ingredients.
   Add all of the ingredients mentioned previously in the list.
   Close after placing the pan in the Cuisinart Bread Machine.
2. **Select the Bake cycle**
   Turn on the Cuisinart Bread Machine. Select the White/Basic setting, select the loaf size, and the crust color. Press start.
   When the cycle is finished, remove the pan from the Cuisinart Bread Machine and let it rest.
   Take the bread out, put in a wire rack to Cool about 5 minutes. Slice

Peanut Butter Bread
PREP: 10 MINUTES /MAKES 1 LOAF

Ingredients
1 cup peanut butter
1 cup milk, at 70°F to 80°F
½ cup packed light brown sugar
¼ cup sugar
¼ cup (½ stick) butter, at room temperature
1 egg, at room temperature
2 teaspoons pure vanilla extract
2 cups all-purpose flour
1 tablespoon baking powder
½ teaspoon salt

Directions
1. **Preparing the Ingredients.**
   Place the peanut butter, milk, brown sugar, sugar, butter, egg, and vanilla in your bread machine.
2. **Select the Bake cycle**
   Set the machine for Quick/Rapid bread and press Start.
   While the wet ingredients are mixing, stir together the flour, baking powder, and salt in a small bowl.
   After the first fast mixing is done, add the dry ingredients.
   When the cycle is finished, remove the pan from the Cuisinart Bread Machine and let it rest.
   Take the bread out, put in a wire rack to Cool about 5 minutes. Slice

Toasted Hazelnut Bread
PREP: 10 MINUTES / MAKES 1 LOAF

Ingredients
12 slice bread (1½ pounds)
1 cup milk, at 70°F to 80°F
1 egg, at room temperature
3¾ tablespoons melted butter, cooled
3 tablespoons honey
¾ teaspoon pure vanilla extract
¾ teaspoon salt
¾ cup finely ground toasted hazelnuts
3 cups white bread flour
1½ teaspoons bread machine or instant yeast

Directions
1. **Preparing the Ingredients.**
   Choose the size of loaf of your preference and then measure the ingredients.
   Add all of the ingredients mentioned previously in the list.
   Close after placing the pan in the Cuisinart Bread Machine.
2. **Select the Bake cycle**
   Turn on the Cuisinart Bread Machine. Select the White/Basic setting, select the loaf size, and the crust color. Press start.
   When the cycle is finished, remove the pan from the Cuisinart Bread Machine and let it rest.
   Take the bread out, put in a wire rack to Cool about 5 minutes. Slice

VEGETABLE BREAD

Potato Honey Bread
PREP: 10 MINUTES /MAKES 1 LOAF

Ingredients
12 slice bread (1½ pounds)
¾ cup lukewarm water
½ cup finely mashed potatoes, at room temperature
1 egg, at room temperature
¼ cup unsalted butter, melted
2 tablespoons honey
1 teaspoon table salt
3 cups white bread flour
2 teaspoons bread machine yeast

Directions
1. **Preparing the Ingredients.**
   Choose the size of loaf of your preference and then measure the ingredients.
   Add all of the ingredients mentioned previously in the list.
   Close after placing the pan in the Cuisinart Bread Machine.
2. **Select the Bake cycle**
   Turn on the Cuisinart Bread Machine. Select the White/Basic setting, select the loaf size, and the crust color. Press start.
   When the cycle is finished, remove the pan from the Cuisinart Bread Machine and let it rest.
   Take the bread out, put in a wire rack to Cool about 10 minutes. Slice

Mashed Potato Bread
PREP: 10 MINUTES /MAKES 1 LOAF

Ingredients
12 slice bread (1½ pounds)
¾ cup water, at 80°F to 90°F
½ cup finely mashed potatoes, at room temperature
1 egg, at room temperature
¼ cup melted butter, cooled
2 tablespoons honey
1 teaspoon salt
3 cups white bread flour
2 teaspoons bread machine or instant yeast

Directions
1. **Preparing the Ingredients.**
   Choose the size of loaf of your preference and then measure the ingredients.
   Add all of the ingredients mentioned previously in the list.
   Close after placing the pan in the Cuisinart Bread Machine.
2. **Select the Bake cycle**
   Turn on the Cuisinart Bread Machine. Select the White/Basic setting, select the loaf size, and the crust color. Press start.
   When the cycle is finished, remove the pan from the Cuisinart Bread Machine and let it rest.
   Take the bread out, put in a wire rack to Cool about 10 minutes. Slice

Dilly Onion Bread
PREP: 10 MINUTES / MAKES 14 SLICES

Ingredients
- ¾ cup water (70°F to 80°F)
- 1 Tbsp butter, softened
- 2 Tbsp sugar
- 3 Tbsp dried minced onion
- 2 Tbsp dried parsley flakes
- 1 Tbsp dill weed
- 1 tsp salt
- 1 garlic clove, minced
- 2 cups bread flour
- ⅓ cup whole wheat flour
- 1 Tbsp nonfat dry milk powder
- 2 tsp active dry yeast serving

Directions

1. **Preparing the Ingredients.**
   Add each ingredient to the Cuisinart Bread Machine in the order and at the temperature recommended by your bread machine manufacturer.
2. **Select the Bake cycle**
   Close, select the basic bread, medium crust setting on your bread machine and press start.
   When the Cuisinart Bread Machine has finished baking, remove the bread and put it on a cooling rack.

Onion Chive Bread
PREP: 10 MINUTES / MAKES 1 LOAF

Ingredients
- 12 slice bread (1½ pounds)
- 1 cup lukewarm water
- 3 tablespoons unsalted butter, melted
- 1½ tablespoons sugar
- 1⅛ teaspoons table salt
- 3⅛ cups white bread flour
- 3 tablespoons dried minced onion
- 1½ tablespoons fresh chives, chopped
- 1⅔ teaspoons bread machine yeast

Directions

1. **Preparing the Ingredients.**
   Choose the size of loaf of your preference and then measure the ingredients.
   Add all of the ingredients mentioned previously in the list.
   Close after placing the pan in the Cuisinart Bread Machine.
2. **Select the Bake cycle**
   Turn on the Cuisinart Bread Machine. Select the White/Basic setting, select the loaf size, and the crust color. Press start.
   When the cycle is finished, remove the pan from the Cuisinart Bread Machine and let it rest.
   Take the bread out, put in a wire rack to Cool about 10 minutes. Slice

Basil Tomato Bread
PREP: 10 MINUTES /MAKES 14 SLICES

Ingredients

2¼ tsp dried active baking yeast
1⅝ cups bread flour
3 Tbsp wheat bran
5 Tbsp quinoa
3 Tbsp dried milk powder
1 Tbsp dried basil
25g sun-dried tomatoes, chopped
1 tsp salt
1⅛ cups water
1 cup boiling water to cover tomatoes

Directions
1. **Preparing the Ingredients.**
   Cover dried tomatoes with boiling water in a bowl.
   Soak for 10 minutes, drain, and cool to room temperature.
   Snip tomatoes into small pieces, using scissors.
   Add each ingredient to the Cuisinart Bread Machine in the order and at the temperature recommended by your bread machine manufacturer.
2. **Select the Bake cycle**
   Close, select the basic bread, medium crust setting on your bread machine and press start.
   When the Cuisinart Bread Machine has finished baking, remove the bread and put it on a cooling rack.

Confetti Bread
PREP: 10 MINUTES /MAKES 1 LOAF

Ingredients

8 slice bread (1 pounds)
⅓ cup milk, at 80°F to 90°F
2 tablespoons water, at 80°F to 90°F
2 teaspoons melted butter, cooled
⅔ teaspoon white vinegar
4 teaspoons sugar
⅔ teaspoon salt
4 teaspoons grated Parmesan cheese
⅓ cup quick oats
1⅔ cups white bread flour
1 teaspoon bread machine or instant yeast
⅓ cup finely chopped zucchini
¼ cup finely chopped yellow bell pepper
¼ cup finely chopped red bell pepper
4 teaspoons chopped chives

Directions
1. **Preparing the Ingredients.**
   Place the ingredients, except the vegetables, in your bread machine as recommended by the manufacturer.
2. **Select the Bake cycle**
   Set the machine for Basic/White bread, select light or medium crust, and press Start.
   When the machine signals, add the chopped vegetables; if your machine has no signal, add the vegetables just before the second kneading is finished.
   When the cycle is finished, remove the pan from the Cuisinart Bread Machine and let it rest.
   Take the bread out, put in a wire rack to Cool about 10 minutes. Slice

Honey Potato Flakes Bread
PREP: 10 MINUTES /MAKES 1 LOAF

Ingredients
12 slice bread (1½ pounds)
1¼ cups lukewarm milk
2 tablespoons unsalted butter, melted
1 tablespoon honey
1½ teaspoons table salt
3 cups white bread flour
1 teaspoon dried thyme
½ cup instant potato flakes
2 teaspoons bread machine yeast

Directions
1. **Preparing the Ingredients.**
   Choose the size of loaf of your preference and then measure the ingredients.
   Add all of the ingredients mentioned previously in the list.
   Close after placing the pan in the Cuisinart Bread Machine.
3. **Select the Bake cycle**
   Turn on the Cuisinart Bread Machine. Select the White/Basic setting, select the loaf size, and the crust color. Press start.
   When the cycle is finished, remove the pan from the Cuisinart Bread Machine and let it rest.
   Take the bread out, put in a wire rack to Cool about 10 minutes. Slice

Pretty Borscht Bread
PREP: 10 MINUTES /MAKES 1 LOAF

Ingredients
12 slice bread (1½ pounds)
¾ cups water, at 80°F to 90°F
¾ cup grated raw beetroot
1½ tablespoons melted butter, cooled
1½ tablespoons sugar
1¼ teaspoons salt
3 cups white bread flour
1¼ teaspoons bread machine or instant yeast

Directions
1. **Preparing the Ingredients.**

Place the ingredients in your bread maker as recommended by the manufacturer.
Set the machine for Basic/White bread, select light or medium crust, and press Start.

2. **Select the Bake cycle**

When the bread is done, remove the bucket from the machine.
Let the loaf cool for 5 minutes.
Gently shake the bucket to remove the loaf, and turn it out onto a rack to cool.

Zucchini Lemon Bread
PREP: 10 MINUTES / MAKES 1 LOAF

Ingredients

12 slice bread (1½ pounds)
½ cup lukewarm milk
¾ cup finely shredded zucchini
¼ teaspoon lemon juice, at room temperature
1 tablespoon olive oil
1 tablespoon sugar
1 teaspoon table salt
¾ cup whole-wheat flour
1½ cups white bread flour
¾ cup quick oats
2¼ teaspoons bread machine yeast

Directions
1. **Preparing the Ingredients.**
    Choose the size of loaf of your preference and then measure the ingredients.
    Add all of the ingredients mentioned previously in the list.
    Close after placing the pan in the Cuisinart Bread Machine.
2. **Select the Bake cycle**
    Turn on the Cuisinart Bread Machine. Select the White/Basic setting, select the loaf size, and the crust color. Press start.
    When the cycle is finished, remove the pan from the Cuisinart Bread Machine and let it rest.
    Take the bread out, put in a wire rack to Cool about 10 minutes. Slice

Yeasted Pumpkin Bread
PREP: 10 MINUTES / MAKES 1 LOAF

Ingredients

8 slice bread (1 pounds)
⅓ cup milk, at 80°F to 90°F
⅔ cup canned pumpkin
2 tablespoons melted butter, cooled
⅔ teaspoon grated ginger
2¾ tablespoons sugar
½ teaspoon salt
⅔ teaspoon ground cinnamon
¼ teaspoon ground cloves
2 cups white bread flour
1⅛ teaspoons bread machine or instant yeast

Directions
1. **Preparing the Ingredients.**
    Choose the size of loaf of your preference and then measure the ingredients.
    Add all of the ingredients mentioned previously in the list.
    Close after placing the pan in the Cuisinart Bread Machine.
2. **Select the Bake cycle**
    Turn on the Cuisinart Bread Machine. Select the White/Basic setting, select the loaf size, and the crust color. Press start.
    When the cycle is finished, remove the pan from the Cuisinart Bread Machine and let it rest.
    Take the bread out, put in a wire rack to Cool about 10 minutes. Slice

Oatmeal Zucchini Bread
PREP: 10 MINUTES / MAKES 1 LOAF

Ingredients
8 slice bread (1 pounds)
⅓ cup milk, at 80°F to 90°F
½ cup finely shredded zucchini
¼ teaspoon freshly squeezed lemon juice, at room temperature
2 teaspoons olive oil
2 teaspoons sugar
⅔ teaspoon salt
½ cup quick oats
½ cup whole-wheat flour
1 cup white bread flour
1½ teaspoons bread machine or instant yeast

Directions
1. **Preparing the Ingredients.**
   Choose the size of loaf of your preference and then measure the ingredients.
   Add all of the ingredients mentioned previously in the list.
   Close after placing the pan in the Cuisinart Bread Machine.
2. **Select the Bake cycle**
   Turn on the Cuisinart Bread Machine. Select the White/Basic setting, select the loaf size, and the crust color. Press start.
   When the cycle is finished, remove the pan from the Cuisinart Bread Machine and let it rest.
   Take the bread out, put in a wire rack to Cool about 10 minutes. Slice

Hot Red Pepper Bread
PREP: 10 MINUTES / MAKES 1 LOAF

Ingredients
12 slice bread (1½ pounds)
1¼ cups milk, at 80°F to 90°F
¼ cup red pepper relish
2 tablespoons chopped roasted red pepper
3 tablespoons melted butter, cooled
3 tablespoons light brown sugar
1 teaspoon salt
3 cups white bread flour
1½ teaspoons bread machine or instant yeast

Directions
1. **Preparing the Ingredients.**
   Choose the size of loaf of your preference and then measure the ingredients.
   Add all of the ingredients mentioned previously in the list.
   Close after placing the pan in the Cuisinart Bread Machine.
2. **Select the Bake cycle**
   Turn on the Cuisinart Bread Machine. Select the White/Basic setting, select the loaf size, and the crust color. Press start.
   When the cycle is finished, remove the pan from the Cuisinart Bread Machine and let it rest.
   Take the bread out, put in a wire rack to Cool about 10 minutes. Slice

French Onion Bread
PREP: 10 MINUTES /MAKES 1 LOAF

Ingredients
12 slice bread (1½ pounds)
1¼ cups milk, at 80°F to 90°F
¼ cup melted butter, cooled
3 tablespoons light brown sugar
1 teaspoon salt
3 tablespoons dehydrated onion flakes
2 tablespoons chopped fresh chives
1 teaspoon garlic powder
3 cups white bread flour
1 teaspoon bread machine or instant yeast

Directions
1. **Preparing the Ingredients.**
   Choose the size of loaf of your preference and then measure the ingredients.
   Add all of the ingredients mentioned previously in the list.
   Close after placing the pan in the Cuisinart Bread Machine.
2. **Select the Bake cycle**
   Turn on the Cuisinart Bread Machine. Select the White/Basic setting, select the loaf size, and the crust color. Press start.
   When the cycle is finished, remove the pan from the Cuisinart Bread Machine and let it rest.
   Take the bread out, put in a wire rack to Cool about 5 minutes. Slice

Golden Butternut Squash Raisin Bread
PREP: 10 MINUTES /MAKES 1 LOAF

Ingredients
16 slice bread (2 pounds)
2 cups cooked mashed butternut squash, at room temperature
1 cup (2 sticks) butter, at room temperature
3 eggs, at room temperature
1 teaspoon pure vanilla extract
2 cups sugar
½ cup light brown sugar
3 cups all-purpose flour
1 teaspoon baking soda
1 teaspoon ground cinnamon
½ teaspoon ground cloves
½ teaspoon ground nutmeg
½ teaspoon salt
½ teaspoon baking powder
½ cup golden raisins

Directions
1. **Preparing the Ingredients.**
   Place the butternut squash, butter, eggs, vanilla, sugar, and brown sugar in your bread machine.
2. **Select the Bake cycle**
   Set the machine for Quick/Rapid bread and press Start.
   While the wet ingredients are mixing, stir together the flour, baking soda, cinnamon, cloves, nutmeg, salt, and baking powder in a small bowl.
   After the first fast mixing is done, add the dry ingredients and raisins.
   When the cycle is finished, remove the pan from the Cuisinart Bread Machine and let it rest.
   Take the bread out, put in a wire rack to Cool about 5 minutes. Slice

Sweet Potato Bread

PREP: 10 MINUTES / MAKES 1 LOAF

Ingredients

12 to 16 slices (1½ to 2 pounds)

1½ cups mashed cooked sweet potato, at room temperature

¾ cup buttermilk, at room temperature

½ cup sugar

¼ cup melted butter, cooled

1 egg, at room temperature

1½ cups all-purpose flour

1 teaspoon ground cinnamon

½ teaspoon baking powder

½ teaspoon baking soda

¼ teaspoon ground cloves

¼ teaspoon salt

Directions

1. **Preparing the Ingredients.**
   Place the sweet potato, buttermilk, sugar, butter, and egg in your bread machine.
2. **Select the Bake cycle**
   Set the machine for Quick/Rapid bread and press Start. While the wet ingredients are mixing, stir together the flour, cinnamon, baking powder, baking soda, cloves, and salt in a small bowl.
   After the first fast mixing is done, add the dry ingredients.
   When the cycle is finished, remove the pan from the Cuisinart Bread Machine and let it rest.
   Take the bread out, put in a wire rack to Cool about 5 minutes. Slice

CHEESE BREADS

Jalapeno Cheddar Bread
PREP: 10 MINUTES /MAKES 1 LOAF

Ingredients
12 slice bread (1½ pounds)
1 cup lukewarm buttermilk
¼ cup unsalted butter, melted
2 eggs, at room temperature
½ teaspoon table salt
1 jalapeno pepper, chopped
½ cup Cheddar cheese, shredded
¼ cup sugar
1⅓ cups all-purpose flour
1 cup cornmeal
1 tablespoon baking powder

Directions
1. **Preparing the Ingredients.**
   Choose the size of loaf of your preference and then measure the ingredients.
   Add all of the ingredients mentioned previously in the list.
   Close after placing the pan in the Cuisinart Bread Machine.
2. **Select the Bake cycle**
   Turn on the Cuisinart Bread Machine. Select the Rapid/Quick setting, select the loaf size, and the crust color. Press start.
   When the cycle is finished, remove the pan from the Cuisinart Bread Machine and let it rest.
   Take the bread out, put in a wire rack to Cool about 5 minutes. Slice

Oregano Cheese Bread
PREP: 10 MINUTES /MAKES 1 LOAF

Ingredients
3 cups bread flour
1 cup water
½ cup freshly grated parmesan cheese
3 Tbsp sugar
1 Tbsp dried leaf oregano
1½ Tbsp olive oil
1 tsp salt
2 tsp active dry yeast

Directions
1. **Preparing the Ingredients**
   Add each ingredient to the Cuisinart Bread Machine in the order and at the temperature recommended by your bread machine manufacturer.
2. **Select the Bake cycle**
   Close, select the basic bread, medium crust setting on your bread machine, and press start.
   When the Cuisinart Bread Machine has finished baking, remove the bread and put it on a cooling rack.

Cheddar Cheese Basil Bread
PREP: 10 MINUTES / MAKES 1 LOAF

Ingredients
12 slice bread (1½ pounds)
1 cup milk, at 80°F to 90°F
1 tablespoon melted butter, cooled
1 tablespoon sugar
1 teaspoon dried basil
¾ cup (3 ounces) shredded sharp Cheddar cheese
¾ teaspoon salt
3 cups white bread flour
1½ teaspoons bread machine or active dry yeast

Directions
1. **Preparing the Ingredients.**
   Choose the size of loaf of your preference and then measure the ingredients.
   Add all of the ingredients mentioned previously in the list.
   Close after placing the pan in the Cuisinart Bread Machine.
2. **Select the Bake cycle**
   Turn on the Cuisinart Bread Machine. Select the White/Basic setting, select the loaf size, and the crust color. Press start.
   When the cycle is finished, remove the pan from the Cuisinart Bread Machine and let it rest.
   Take the bread out, put in a wire rack to Cool about 5 minutes. Slice

Spinach and Feta Bread
PREP: 10 MINUTES / MAKES 14 SLICES

Ingredients
1 cup water
2 tsp butter
3 cups flour
1 tsp sugar
2 tsp instant minced onion
1 tsp salt
1¼ tsp instant yeast
1 cup crumbled feta
1 cup chopped fresh spinach leaves

Directions
1. **Preparing the Ingredients**
   Add each ingredient except the cheese and spinach to the Cuisinart Bread Machine in the order and at the temperature recommended by your bread machine manufacturer.

2. **Select the Bake cycle**
   Close, select the basic bread, medium crust setting on your bread machine, and press start.
   When only 10 minutes are left in the last kneading cycle add the spinach and cheese.
   When the Cuisinart Bread Machine has finished baking, remove the bread and put it on a cooling rack.

Blue Cheese Bread
PREP: 10 MINUTES / MAKES 12 SLICES

Ingredients

3/4 cup warm water
1 large egg
1 teaspoon salt
3 cups bread flour
1 cup blue cheese, crumbled
2 tablespoons nonfat dry milk
2 tablespoons sugar
1 teaspoon bread machine yeast

Directions
1. **Preparing the Ingredients**
   Add the ingredients to bread machine pan in the order listed above, (except yeast) ; be sure to add the cheese with the flour.
   Make a well in the flour; pour the yeast into the hole.

2. **Select the Bake cycle**
   Select Basic bread cycle, medium crust color, and press Start.
   When finished, transfer to a cooling rack for 10 minutes and serve warm.

Parsley Garlic Bread
PREP: 10 MINUTES / MAKES 1 LOAF

Ingredients

12 slice bread (1½ pounds)
1 cup lukewarm milk
1½ tablespoons unsalted butter, melted
1 tablespoon sugar
1½ teaspoons table salt
2 teaspoons garlic powder
2 teaspoons fresh parsley, chopped
3 cups white bread flour
1¾ teaspoons bread machine yeast

Directions
1. **Preparing the Ingredients.**
   Choose the size of loaf of your preference and then measure the ingredients.
   Add all of the ingredients mentioned previously in the list.
   Close after placing the pan in the Cuisinart Bread Machine.
2. **Select the Bake cycle**
   Turn on the Cuisinart Bread Machine. Select the White/Basic setting, select the loaf size, and the crust color. Press start.
   When the cycle is finished, remove the pan from the Cuisinart Bread Machine and let it rest.
   Take the bread out, put in a wire rack to Cool about 10 minutes. Slice

Prosciutto Parmesan Breadsticks
PREP: 10 MINUTES / MAKES 12

Ingredients
1 1/3 cups warm water
1 tablespoon butter
1 1/2 tablespoons sugar
1 1/2 teaspoons salt
4 cups bread flour
2 teaspoons yeast
For the topping:
1/2 pound prosciutto, sliced very thin
1/2 cup of grated parmesan cheese
1 egg yolk
1 tablespoon of water

Directions
1. **Preparing the Ingredients**
   Place the first set of dough ingredients (except yeast) in the bread pan in the order indicated. Do not add any of the topping ingredients yet. Make a well in the center of the dry ingredients and add the yeast.
2. **Select the Bake cycle**
   Select the Dough cycle on the Cuisinart Bread Machine. When finished, drop the dough onto a lightly-floured surface. Roll the dough out flat to about 1/4-inch thick, or about half a centimeter. Cover with plastic wrap and let rise for 20 to 30 minutes.
   Sprinkle dough evenly with parmesan and carefully lay the prosciutto slices on the surface of the dough to cover as much of it as possible. Preheat an oven to 400°F.
   Cut the dough into 12 long strips, about one inch wide. Twist each end in opposite directions, twisting the toppings into the bread stick. Place the breadsticks onto a lightly greased baking sheet. Whisk the egg yolk and water together in a small mixing bowl and lightly baste each breadstick. Bake for 8 to 10 minutes or until golden brown.
   Remove from oven and serve warm.

Jalapeño Corn Bread
PREP: 10 MINUTES / MAKES 1 LOAF

Ingredients
12 to 16 slices bread (1½ to 2 pounds)
1 cup buttermilk, at 80°F to 90°F
¼ cup melted butter, cooled
2 eggs, at room temperature
1 jalapeño pepper, chopped
1⅓ cups all-purpose flour
1 cup cornmeal
½ cup (2 ounces) shredded Cheddar cheese
¼ cup sugar
1 tablespoon baking powder
½ teaspoon salt

Directions
1. **Preparing the Ingredients.**
   Choose the size of loaf of your preference and then measure the ingredients.
   Add all of the ingredients mentioned previously in the list.
   Close after placing the pan in the Cuisinart Bread Machine.
2. **Select the Bake cycle**
   Turn on the Cuisinart Bread Machine. Select the Quick/Rapid setting, select the loaf size, and the crust color. Press start.
   When the cycle is finished, remove the pan from the Cuisinart Bread Machine and let it rest.
   Take the bread out, put in a wire rack to Cool about 5 minutes. Slice

Cheddar Bacon Bread
PREP: 10 MINUTES /MAKES 1 LOAF

Ingredients
12 slice bread (1½ pounds)
½ cup lukewarm milk
1½ teaspoons unsalted butter, melted
1½ tablespoons honey
1½ teaspoons table salt
½ cup green chilies, chopped
½ cup grated Cheddar cheese
½ cup cooked bacon, chopped
3 cups white bread flour
2 teaspoons bread machine yeast

Directions
1. **Preparing the Ingredients.**
   Choose the size of loaf of your preference and then measure the ingredients.
   Add all of the ingredients mentioned previously in the list.
   Close after placing the pan in the Cuisinart Bread Machine.

2. **Select the Bake cycle**
   Turn on the Cuisinart Bread Machine. Select the White/Basic setting, select the loaf size, and the crust color. Press start.
   When the cycle is finished, remove the pan from the Cuisinart Bread Machine and let it rest.
   Take the bread out, put in a wire rack to Cool about 5 minutes. Slice

Italian Cheese Bread
PREP: 10 MINUTES /MAKES 14 SLICES

Ingredients
1¼ cups water
3 cups bread flour
½ shredded pepper jack cheese
2 tsp Italian seasoning
2 Tbsp brown sugar
1½ tsp salt
2 tsp active dry yeast

Directions
1. **Preparing the Ingredients.**
   Add each ingredient to the Cuisinart Bread Machine in the order and at the temperature recommended by your bread machine manufacturer.
2. **Select the Bake cycle**
   Close, select the basic bread, medium crust setting on your bread machine, and press start.
   When the Cuisinart Bread Machine has finished baking, remove the bread and put it on a cooling rack.

Olive Cheese Bread
PREP: 10 MINUTES / MAKES 1 LOAF

Ingredients
12 slice bread (1½ pounds)
1 cup milk, at 80°F to 90°F
1½ tablespoons melted butter, cooled
1 teaspoon minced garlic
1½ tablespoons sugar
1 teaspoon salt
3 cups white bread flour
¾ cup (3 ounces) shredded Swiss cheese
1 teaspoon bread machine or instant yeast
⅓ cup chopped black olives

Directions
1. **Preparing the Ingredients.**
   Place the ingredients in your bread maker as recommended by the manufacturer, tossing the flour with the cheese first.
2. **Select the Bake cycle**
   Set the machine for Basic/White bread, select light or medium crust, and press Start.
   When the cycle is finished, remove the pan from the Cuisinart Bread Machine and let it rest.
   Take the bread out, put in a wire rack to Cool about 10 minutes. Slice

Cheesy Sausage Loaf
PREP: 10 MINUTES / MAKES 1 LOAF

Ingredients
1 cup warm water
4 teaspoons butter, softened
1 1/4 teaspoons salt
1 teaspoon sugar
3 cups bread flour
2 1/4 teaspoons active dry yeast
1 pound pork sausage roll, cooked and drained
1 1/2 cups Italian cheese, shredded
1/4 teaspoon garlic powder
Pinch of black pepper
1 egg, lightly beaten
Flour, for surface

Directions
1. **Preparing the Ingredients**
   Add the first five ingredients to the bread maker pan in order listed above.
   Make a well in the flour; pour the yeast into the hole.
2. **Select the Bake cycle**
   Select Dough cycle and press Start.
   Turn kneaded dough onto a lightly floured surface and roll into a 16-by-10-inch rectangle. Cover with plastic wrap and let rest for 10 minutes Combine sausage, cheese, garlic powder and pepper in a mixing bowl.
   Spread sausage mixture evenly over the dough to within one 1/2 inch of edges. Start with a long side and roll up like a jelly roll, pinch seams to seal, and tuck ends under. Place the loaf seam-side down on a greased baking sheet. Cover and let rise in a warm place for 30 minutes. Preheat an oven to 350°F and bake 20 minutes. Brush with egg and bake an additional 15 to 20 minutes until golden brown. Remove to a cooling rack and serve warm.

Mixed Herb Cheese Bread
PREP: 10 MINUTES PLUS FERMENTING TIME/MAKES 1 LOAF

Ingredients
12 slice bread (1½ pounds)
1 cup lukewarm water
1½ tablespoons olive oil
¾ teaspoon table salt
¾ tablespoon sugar
2 cloves garlic, crushed
2 tablespoons mixed fresh herbs (basil, chives, oregano, rosemary, etc.)
3 tablespoons Parmesan cheese, grated
3 cups white bread flour
1⅔ teaspoons bread machine yeast

Directions
1. **Preparing the Ingredients.**
   Choose the size of loaf of your preference and then measure the ingredients.
   Add all of the ingredients mentioned previously in the list.
   Close after placing the pan in the Cuisinart Bread Machine.
2. **Select the Bake cycle**
   Turn on the Cuisinart Bread Machine. Select the White/Basic setting, select the loaf size, and the crust color. Press start.
   When the cycle is finished, remove the pan from the Cuisinart Bread Machine and let it rest.
   Take the bread out, put in a wire rack to Cool about 5 minutes. Slice

Blue Cheese Onion Bread
PREP: 10 MINUTES PLUS FERMENTING TIME /MAKES 1 LOAF

Ingredients
12 slice bread (1½ pounds)
1¼ cup water, at 80°F to 90°F
1 egg, at room temperature
1 tablespoon melted butter, cooled
¼ cup powdered skim milk
1 tablespoon sugar
¾ teaspoon salt
½ cup (2 ounces) crumbled blue cheese
1 tablespoon dried onion flakes
3 cups white bread flour
¼ cup instant mashed potato flakes
1 teaspoon bread machine or active dry yeast

Directions
1. **Preparing the Ingredients.**
   Choose the size of loaf of your preference and then measure the ingredients.
   Add all of the ingredients mentioned previously in the list.
   Close after placing the pan in the Cuisinart Bread Machine.
2. **Select the Bake cycle**
   Turn on the Cuisinart Bread Machine. Select the Quick/Rapid setting, select the loaf size, and the crust color. Press start.
   When the cycle is finished, remove the pan from the Cuisinart Bread Machine and let it rest.
   Take the bread out, put in a wire rack to Cool about 10 minutes. Slice

Cheddar and Bacon Bread

PREP: 10 MINUTES PLUS FERMENTING TIME / MAKES 14 SLICES

Ingredients

1⅓ cups water
2 Tbsp vegetable oil
1¼ tsp salt
2 Tbsp plus 1½ tsp sugar
4 cups bread flour
3 Tbsp nonfat dry milk
2 tsp dry active yeast
2 cups cheddar
8 slices crumbled bacon

Directions

1. **Preparing the Ingredients**
   Add each ingredient to the Cuisinart Bread Machine except the cheese and bacon in the order and at the temperature recommended by your bread machine manufacturer.
2. **Select the Bake cycle**
   Close, select the basic bread, medium crust setting on your bread machine, and press start.
   Add the cheddar cheese and bacon 30 to 40 minutes into the cycle. When the Cuisinart Bread Machine has finished baking, remove the bread and put it on a cooling rack.

Basil Cheese Bread

PREP: 10 MINUTES PLUS FERMENTING TIME / MAKES 1 LOAF

Ingredients

12 slice bread (1½ pounds)
1 cup lukewarm milk
1 tablespoon unsalted butter, melted
1 tablespoon sugar
1 teaspoon dried basil
¾ teaspoon table salt
¾ cup sharp Cheddar cheese, shredded
3 cups white bread flour
1½ teaspoons bread machine yeast

Directions

1. **Preparing the Ingredients.**
   Choose the size of loaf of your preference and then measure the ingredients.
   Add all of the ingredients mentioned previously in the list.
   Close after placing the pan in the Cuisinart Bread Machine.
2. **Select the Bake cycle**
   Turn on the Cuisinart Bread Machine. Select the Quick/Rapid setting, select the loaf size, and the crust color. Press start.
   When the cycle is finished, remove the pan from the Cuisinart Bread Machine and let it rest.
   Take the bread out, put in a wire rack to Cool about 5 minutes. Slice

Double Cheese Bread

PREP: 10 MINUTES PLUS FERMENTING TIME/MAKES 1 LOAF

Ingredients

8 slices bread (1 pound)
¾ cup plus 1 tablespoon milk, at 80°F to 90°F
2 teaspoons butter, melted and cooled
4 teaspoons sugar
⅔ teaspoon salt
⅓ teaspoon freshly ground black pepper
Pinch cayenne pepper
1 cup (4 ounces) shredded aged sharp Cheddar cheese
⅓ cup shredded or grated Parmesan cheese
2 cups white bread flour
¾ teaspoon bread machine or instant yeast

Directions

1. **Preparing the Ingredients.**
   Choose the size of loaf of your preference and then measure the ingredients.
   Add all of the ingredients mentioned previously in the list.
   Close after placing the pan in the Cuisinart Bread Machine.
2. **Select the Bake cycle**
   Turn on the Cuisinart Bread Machine. Select the Quick/Rapid setting, select the loaf size, and the crust color. Press start.
   When the cycle is finished, remove the pan from the Cuisinart Bread Machine and let it rest.
   Take the bread out, put in a wire rack to Cool about 5 minutes. Slice

American Cheese Beer Bread

PREP: 10 MINUTES PLUS FERMENTING TIME /MAKES 1 LOAF

Ingredients

16 slice bread (2 pounds)
1⅔ cups warm beer
1½ tablespoons sugar
2 teaspoons table salt
1½ tablespoons unsalted butter, melted
¾ cup American cheese, shredded
¾ cup Monterrey Jack cheese, shredded
4 cups white bread flour
2 teaspoons bread machine yeast

Directions

1. **Preparing the Ingredients.**
   Choose the size of loaf of your preference and then measure the ingredients.
   Add all of the ingredients mentioned previously in the list.
   Close after placing the pan in the Cuisinart Bread Machine.
2. **Select the Bake cycle**
   Turn on the Cuisinart Bread Machine. Select the Quick/Rapid setting, select the loaf size, and the crust color. Press start.
   When the cycle is finished, remove the pan from the Cuisinart Bread Machine and let it rest.
   Take the bread out, put in a wire rack to Cool about 5 minutes. Slice

Mozzarella and Salami Bread
PREP: 10 MINUTES PLUS FERMENTING TIME /MAKES 1 LOAF

Ingredients
12 slice bread (1½ pounds)
1 cup water plus 2 tablespoons, at 80°F to 90°F
½ cup (2 ounces) shredded mozzarella cheese
2 tablespoons sugar
1 teaspoon salt
1 teaspoon dried basil
¼ teaspoon garlic powder
3¼ cups white bread flour
1½ teaspoons bread machine or instant yeast
¾ cup finely diced hot German salami

Directions
1. **Preparing the Ingredients.**

Place the ingredients, except the salami, in your bread machine as recommended by the manufacturer. Set the machine for Basic/White bread, select light or medium crust, and press Start. When the bread is done, remove the bucket from the machine.

2. **Select the Bake cycle**

Add the salami when your machine signals or 5 minutes before the second kneading cycle is finished. Let the loaf cool for 5 minutes. Gently shake the bucket to remove the loaf, and turn it out onto a rack to cool.

Simple Cottage Cheese Bread
PREP: 10 MINUTES PLUS FERMENTING TIME /MAKES 1 LOAF

Ingredients
12 slice bread (1½ pounds)
½ cup water, at 80°F to 90°F
¾ cup cottage cheese, at room temperature
1 egg, at room temperature
2 tablespoons butter, melted and cooled
1 tablespoon sugar
1 teaspoon salt
¼ teaspoon baking soda
3 cups white bread flour
2 teaspoons bread machine or instant yeast

Directions
1. **Preparing the Ingredients.**
   Choose the size of loaf of your preference and then measure the ingredients.
   Add all of the ingredients mentioned previously in the list.
   Close after placing the pan in the Cuisinart Bread Machine.
2. **Select the Bake cycle**
   Turn on the Cuisinart Bread Machine. Select the White/Basic setting, select the loaf size, and the crust color. Press start.
   When the cycle is finished, remove the pan from the Cuisinart Bread Machine and let it rest.
   Take the bread out, put in a wire rack to Cool about 5 minutes. Slice

SWEET BREAD

Swedish Coffee Bread
PREP: 10 MINUTES / MAKES 14 SLICES

Ingredients
1 cup milk
½ tsp salt
1 egg yolk
2 Tbsp softened butter
3 cups all-purpose flour
⅓ cup sugar
1 envelope active dry yeast
3 tsp ground cardamom
2 egg whites, slightly beaten

Directions
1. **Preparing the Ingredients**
   Add each ingredient to the Cuisinart Bread Machine in the order and at the temperature recommended by your bread machine manufacturer.
2. **Select the Bake cycle**
   Select the dough cycle and press start. Grease your baking sheet.
   When the dough cycle has finished, divide the dough into three equal parts. Roll each part into a rope 12-14" long. Lay 3 ropes side by side, and then braid them together.
   Tuck the ends underneath and put onto the sheet. Next, cover the bread, using kitchen towel, and let it rise until it has doubled in size. Brush your bread with beaten egg white and sprinkle with pearl sugar. Bake until golden brown at 375°F in a preheated oven for 20-25 minutes. When baked, remove the bread and put it on a cooling rack.

Pear Kuchen with Ginger Topping
PREP: 20 MINUTES PLUS FERMENTING TIME / MAKES 12 SERVINGS

Ingredients
Bread dough
½ cup milk
2 tablespoons butter, softened
1 egg
2 cups bread flour
2 tablespoons sugar
1 teaspoon salt
1¾ teaspoons bread machine or fast-acting dry yeast

Topping
3 cups sliced peeled pears
1 cup sugar
2 tablespoons butter, softened
1 tablespoon chopped crystallized ginger
½ cup whipping cream
1 egg yolk

Directions
1. **Preparing the Ingredients.**
Measure carefully, placing all bread dough ingredients in bread machine pan in the order recommended by the manufacturer.
2. **Select the Bake cycle**
Select Dough/Manual cycle. Do not use delay cycle.
Remove dough from pan, using lightly floured hands. Cover and let rest 10 minutes on lightly floured surface.
Grease 13×9-inch pan with shortening. Press dough evenly in bottom of pan.

Arrange pears on dough. In small bowl, mix 1 cup sugar, 2 tablespoons butter and the ginger. Reserve 2 tablespoons of the topping; sprinkle remaining topping over pears. Cover and let rise in warm place 30 to 45 minutes or until doubled in size. Dough is ready if indentation remains when touched.

Heat oven to 375°F. Bake 20 minutes. Mix whipping cream and egg yolk; pour over hot kuchen. Bake 15 minutes longer or until golden brown. Sprinkle with reserved 2 tablespoons topping. Serve warm.

Walnut Cocoa Bread
PREP: 20 MINUTES PLUS FERMENTING TIME /MAKES 14 SERVINGS

Ingredients
⅔ cup milk
⅓ cup water
5 Tbsp butter, softened
⅓ cup packed brown sugar
5 Tbsp baking cocoa
1 tsp salt
3 cups bread flour
2¼ tsp active dry yeast
⅔ cup chopped walnuts, toasted

Directions
1. **Preparing the Ingredients**
   Add each ingredient except the walnuts to the Cuisinart Bread Machine in the order and at the temperature recommended by your bread machine manufacturer.
2. **Select the Bake cycle**
   Close, select the sweet loaf, low crust setting on your bread machine, and press start.
   Just before the final kneading, add the walnuts.
   When the Cuisinart Bread Machine has finished baking, remove the bread and put it on a cooling rack.

Sweet Applesauce Bread
PREP: 10 MINUTES PLUS FERMENTING TIME /MAKES 1 LOAF

Ingredients
12 slice bread (1½ pounds)
⅔ cup lukewarm milk
¼ cup unsweetened applesauce, at room temperature
1 tablespoon unsalted butter, melted
1 tablespoon sugar
1 teaspoon table salt
¼ cup quick oats
2¼ cups white bread flour
½ teaspoon ground cinnamon
Pinch ground nutmeg
2¼ teaspoons bread machine yeast

Directions
1. **Preparing the Ingredients.**
   Choose the size of loaf of your preference and then measure the ingredients.
   Add all of the ingredients mentioned previously in the list.
   Close after placing the pan in the Cuisinart Bread Machine.
2. **Select the Bake cycle**
   Turn on the Cuisinart Bread Machine. Select the Quick/Rapid setting, select the loaf size, and the crust color. Press start.
   When the cycle is finished, remove the pan from the Cuisinart Bread Machine and let it rest.
   Take the bread out, put in a wire rack to Cool about 5 minutes. Slice

Mexican Chocolate Bread
PREP: 10 MINUTES PLUS FERMENTING TIME /MAKES 1 LOAF

Ingredients
½ cup milk
½ cup orange juice
1 large egg plus 1 egg yolk
3 Tbsp unsalted butter cut into pieces
2½ cups bread flour
¼ cup light brown sugar
3 Tbsp unsweetened dutch-process cocoa powder
1 Tbsp gluten
1 tsp instant espresso powder
¾ tsp ground cinnamon
½ cup bittersweet chocolate chips
2½ tsp bread machine yeast

Directions
1. **Preparing the Ingredients.**
   Add each ingredient to the Cuisinart Bread Machine in the order and at the temperature recommended by your bread machine manufacturer.
2. **Select the Bake cycle**
   Close, select the sweet loaf, low crust setting on your bread machine, and press start.
   When the Cuisinart Bread Machine has finished baking, remove the bread and put it on a cooling rack.

Sour Cream Maple Bread
PREP: 10 MINUTES PLUS FERMENTING TIME /MAKES 1 LOAF

Ingredients
8 slices bread (1 pound)
6 tablespoons water, at 80°F to 90°F
6 tablespoons sour cream, at room temperature
1½ tablespoons butter, at room temperature
¾ tablespoon maple syrup
½ teaspoon salt
1¾ cups white bread flour
1⅛ teaspoons bread machine or instant yeast

Directions
1. **Preparing the Ingredients.**
   Choose the size of loaf of your preference and then measure the ingredients.
   Add all of the ingredients mentioned previously in the list.
   Close after placing the pan in the Cuisinart Bread Machine.
2. **Select the Bake cycle**
   Turn on the Cuisinart Bread Machine. Select the Quick/Rapid setting, select the loaf size, and the crust color. Press start.
   When the cycle is finished, remove the pan from the Cuisinart Bread Machine and let it rest.
   Take the bread out, put in a wire rack to Cool about 5 minutes. Slice

Chocolate Chip Bread
PREP: 10 MINUTES PLUS FERMENTING TIME /MAKES 1 LOAF

Ingredients
¼ cup water
1 cup milk
1 egg
3 cups bread flour
3 Tbsp brown sugar
2 Tbsp white sugar
1 tsp salt
1 tsp ground cinnamon
1½ tsp active dry yeast
2 Tbsp margarine, softened
¾ cup semisweet chocolate chips

Directions
1. **Preparing the Ingredients**
   Add each ingredient except the chocolate chips to the Cuisinart Bread Machine in the order and at the temperature recommended by your bread machine manufacturer.
2. **Select the Bake cycle**
   Close, select the sweet loaf, low crust setting on your bread machine, and press start.
   Add the chocolate chips about 5 minutes before the kneading cycle has finished. When the Cuisinart Bread Machine has finished baking, remove the bread and put it on a cooling rack.

Milk Sweet Bread
PREP: 10 MINUTES PLUS FERMENTING TIME /MAKES 1 LOAF

Ingredients
12 slice bread (1½ pounds)
1 cup lukewarm milk
1 egg, at room temperature
2 tablespoons butter, softened
½ cup sugar
1 teaspoon table salt
3 cups white bread flour
2¼ teaspoons bread machine yeast

Directions
1. **Preparing the Ingredients.**
   Choose the size of loaf of your preference and then measure the ingredients.
   Add all of the ingredients mentioned previously in the list.
   Close after placing the pan in the Cuisinart Bread Machine.
2. **Select the Bake cycle**
   Turn on the Cuisinart Bread Machine. Select the Sweet setting, select the loaf size, and the crust color. Press start.
   When the cycle is finished, remove the pan from the Cuisinart Bread Machine and let it rest.
   Take the bread out, put in a wire rack to Cool about 5 minutes. Slice

Barmbrack Bread
PREP: 10 MINUTES PLUS FERMENTING TIME /MAKES 1 LOAF

Ingredients
8 slices bread (1 pound)
⅔ cup water, at 80°F to 90°F

1 tablespoon melted butter, cooled
2 tablespoons sugar
2 tablespoons skim milk powder
1 teaspoon salt
1 teaspoon dried lemon zest
¼ teaspoon ground allspice
⅛ teaspoon ground nutmeg
2 cups white bread flour
1½ teaspoons bread machine or active dry yeast
½ cup dried currants

Directions
1. **Preparing the Ingredients.**
   Place the ingredients, except the currants, in your bread machine as recommended by the manufacturer.
2. **Select the Bake cycle**
   Set the machine for Basic/White bread, select light or medium crust, and press Start.
   Add the currants when your machine signals or when the second kneading cycle starts. When the cycle is finished, remove the pan from the Cuisinart Bread Machine and let it rest. Take the bread out, put in a wire rack to Cool about 5 minutes. Slice

Pumpernickel Bread
PREP: 10 MINUTES PLUS FERMENTING TIME /MAKES 12 SLICES

Ingredients
1 cup plus 2 tablespoons water
1½ teaspoons salt
1/3 cup molasses
2 tablespoons vegetable oil
1 cup plus 1 tablespoon rye flour
1 cup plus 2 tablespoons whole wheat flour
1½ cups bread flour
3 tablespoons unsweetened baking cocoa
1½ teaspoons instant coffee granules or crystals
1 tablespoon caraway seed
1 teaspoon bread machine or fast-acting dry yeast

Directions
1. **Preparing the Ingredients.**
Measure carefully, placing all ingredients in bread machine pan in the order recommended by the manufacturer.

2. **Select the Bake cycle**
Select Whole Wheat or Basic/White cycle. Use Medium or Light crust color.
Remove baked bread from pan; cool on cooling rack.

Allspice Currant Bread
PREP: 10 MINUTES PLUS FERMENTING TIME /MAKES 1 LOAF

Ingredients
16 slice bread (2 pounds)
1½ cups lukewarm water
2 tablespoons unsalted butter, melted
¼ cup sugar
¼ cup skim milk powder
2 teaspoons table salt
4 cups white bread flour
1½ teaspoons dried lemon zest
¾ teaspoon ground allspice
¼ teaspoon ground nutmeg
2½ teaspoons bread machine yeast
1 cup dried currants

Directions
1. **Preparing the Ingredients.**
   Choose the size of loaf of your preference and then measure the ingredients.
   Add all of the ingredients mentioned previously in the list, except for the dried currants. Close after placing the pan in the Cuisinart Bread Machine.
2. **Select the Bake cycle**
   Press the "Start" button. Select the White/Basic or Fruit/Nut (if your machine has this setting) setting, then the loaf size, and finally the crust color. Start the cycle.
   When the machine signals to add ingredients, add the dried currants.
   When the cycle is finished, remove the pan from the Cuisinart Bread Machine and let it rest. Take the bread out, put in a wire rack to Cool about 5 minutes. Slice

Apple Butter Bread
PREP: 10 MINUTES PLUS FERMENTING TIME /MAKES 1 LOAF

Ingredients
8 slices bread (1 pound)
⅔ cup milk, at 80°F to 90°F
⅓ cup apple butter, at room temperature
4 teaspoons melted butter, cooled
2 teaspoons honey
⅔ teaspoon salt
⅔ cup whole-wheat flour
1½ cups white bread flour
1 teaspoon bread machine or instant yeast

Directions
1. **Preparing the Ingredients.**
   Choose the size of loaf of your preference and then measure the ingredients.
   Add all of the ingredients mentioned previously in the list.
   Close after placing the pan in the Cuisinart Bread Machine.
2. **Select the Bake cycle**
   Turn on the Cuisinart Bread Machine. Select the Quick/Rapid setting, select the loaf size, and the crust color. Press start.
   When the cycle is finished, remove the pan from the Cuisinart Bread Machine and let it rest.
   Take the bread out, put in a wire rack to Cool about 5 minutes. Slice

Beer and Pretzel Bread
PREP: 10 MINUTES PLUS FERMENTING TIME /MAKES 12 SLICES

Ingredients
¾ cup regular or nonalcoholic beer
1/3 cup water
2 tablespoons butter, softened
3 cups bread flour
1 tablespoon packed brown sugar
1 teaspoon ground mustard
1 teaspoon salt
1½ teaspoons bread machine yeast
½ cup bite-size pretzel pieces, about 1×¾ inch, or pretzel rods, cut into 1-inch pieces

Directions
1. **Preparing the Ingredients.**

Measure carefully, placing all ingredients except pretzels in bread machine pan in order recommended by the manufacturer.

2. **Select the Bake cycle**

Select Basic/White cycle. Use Medium or Light crust color. Do not use delay cycle.
Add pretzels 5 minutes before the last kneading cycle ends. Remove baked bread from pan; cool on cooling rack.

Buttermilk Pecan Bread
PREP: 10 MINUTES PLUS FERMENTING TIME / MAKES 1 LOAF

Ingredients
12 slice bread (1½ pounds)
¾ cup buttermilk, at room temperature
¾ cup butter, at room temperature
1 tablespoon instant coffee granules
3 eggs, at room temperature
¾ cup sugar
2 cups all-purpose flour
½ tablespoon baking powder
½ teaspoon table salt
1 cup chopped pecans

Directions
1. **Preparing the Ingredients.**
   Choose the size of loaf of your preference and then measure the ingredients.
   Add all of the ingredients mentioned previously in the list.
   Close after placing the pan in the Cuisinart Bread Machine.
2. **Select the Bake cycle**
   Turn on the Cuisinart Bread Machine. Select the Quick/Rapid setting, select the loaf size, and the crust color. Press start.
   When the cycle is finished, remove the pan from the Cuisinart Bread Machine and let it rest.
   Take the bread out, put in a wire rack to Cool about 5 minutes. Slice

Crusty Honey Bread
PREP: 10 MINUTES PLUS FERMENTING TIME / MAKES 1 LOAF

Ingredients
12 slice bread (1½ pounds)
1 cup minus 1 tablespoon water, at 80°F to 90°F
1½ tablespoons honey
1⅛ tablespoons melted butter, cooled
¾ teaspoon salt
2⅔ cups white bread flour
1½ teaspoons bread machine or instant yeast

Directions
1. **Preparing the Ingredients.**
   Choose the size of loaf of your preference and then measure the ingredients.
   Add all of the ingredients mentioned previously in the list.
   Close after placing the pan in the Cuisinart Bread Machine.
2. **Select the Bake cycle**
   Turn on the Cuisinart Bread Machine. Select the Basic/White setting, select the loaf size, and the crust color. Press start.
   When the cycle is finished, remove the pan from the Cuisinart Bread Machine and let it rest.
   Take the bread out, put in a wire rack to Cool about 5 minutes. Slice

Brown Sugar Date Nut Swirl Bread
PREP: 10 MINUTES PLUS FERMENTING TIME / MAKES 1 LOAF

Ingredients
1 cup milk
1 large egg
4 tablespoons butter
4 tablespoons sugar
1 teaspoon salt
4 cups flour
1 2/3 teaspoons yeast
For the filling:
1/2 cup packed brown sugar
1 cup walnuts, chopped
1 cup medjool dates, pitted and chopped
2 teaspoons cinnamon
2 teaspoons clove spice
1 1/3 tablespoons butter
Powdered sugar, sifted

Directions
1. **Preparing the Ingredients**
   Add wet ingredients to the bread maker pan. Mix flour, sugar and salt and add to pan.
   Make a well in the center of the dry ingredients and add the yeast.
2. **Select the Bake cycle**
   Select the Dough cycle and press Start. Punch the dough down and allow it to rest in a warm place.
   Mix the brown sugar with walnuts, dates and spices; set aside. Roll the dough into a rectangle, on a lightly floured surface. Baste with a tablespoon of butter, add the filling. Start from the short side and roll the dough to form a jelly roll shape. Place the roll into a greased loaf pan and cover. Let it rise in a warm place, until nearly doubled in size; about 30 minutes. Bake at 350°F for approximately 30 minutes. Cover with foil during the last 10 minutes of cooking. Transfer to a cooling rack for 15 minutes; sprinkle with the powdered sugar and serve.

Cashew Butter/Peanut Butter Bread
PREP: 10 MINUTES PLUS FERMENTING TIME / MAKES 1 LOAF

Ingredients
12 slice bread (1½ pounds)
1 cup peanut butter or cashew butter
1 cup lukewarm milk
½ cup packed light brown sugar
¼ cup sugar
¼ cup butter, at room temperature
1 egg, at room temperature
2 teaspoons pure vanilla extract
2 cups all-purpose flour
1 tablespoon baking powder
½ teaspoon table salt

Directions
1. **Preparing the Ingredients.**
   Choose the size of loaf of your preference and then measure the ingredients. Add all of the ingredients mentioned previously in the list. Close after placing the pan in the Cuisinart Bread Machine.
2. **Select the Bake cycle**
   Turn on the Cuisinart Bread Machine. Select the Quick/Rapid setting, select the loaf size, and the crust color. Press start. When the cycle is finished, remove the pan from the Cuisinart Bread Machine and let it rest.
   Take the bread out, put in a wire rack to Cool about 5 minutes. Slice

Honey Granola Bread

PREP: 10 MINUTES PLUS FERMENTING TIME /MAKES 1 LOAF

Ingredients
12 slice bread (1½ pounds)
1⅛ cups milk, at 80°F to 90°F
3 tablespoons honey
1½ tablespoons butter, melted and cooled
1⅛ teaspoons salt
¾ cup whole-wheat flour
⅔ cup prepared granola, crushed
1¾ cups white bread flour
1½ teaspoons bread machine or instant yeast

Directions
1. **Preparing the Ingredients.**
   Choose the size of loaf of your preference and then measure the ingredients.
   Add all of the ingredients mentioned previously in the list.
   Close after placing the pan in the Cuisinart Bread Machine.
2. **Select the Bake cycle**
   Turn on the Cuisinart Bread Machine. Select the Basic/White setting, select the loaf size, and the crust color. Press start.
   When the cycle is finished, remove the pan from the Cuisinart Bread Machine and let it rest.
   Take the bread out, put in a wire rack to Cool about 5 minutes. Slice

Delicious Sour Cream Bread

PREP: 10 MINUTES PLUS FERMENTING TIME /MAKES 1 LOAF

Ingredients
12 slice bread (1½ pounds)
½ cup + 1 tablespoon lukewarm water
½ cup + 1 tablespoon sour cream, at room temperature
2¼ tablespoons butter, at room temperature
1 tablespoon maple syrup
¾ teaspoon table salt
2¾ cups white bread flour
1⅔ teaspoons bread machine yeast

Directions
1. **Preparing the Ingredients.**
   Choose the size of loaf of your preference and then measure the ingredients.
   Add all of the ingredients mentioned previously in the list.
   Close after placing the pan in the Cuisinart Bread Machine.
2. **Select the Bake cycle**
   Turn on the Cuisinart Bread Machine. Select the Basic/White setting, select the loaf size, and the crust color. Press start.
   When the cycle is finished, remove the pan from the Cuisinart Bread Machine and let it rest.
   Take the bread out, put in a wire rack to Cool about 5 minutes. Slice

Black Bread
PREP: 10 MINUTES PLUS FERMENTING TIME /MAKES 1 LOAF

Ingredients
12 slice bread (1½ pounds)
¾ cup water, at 80°F to 90°F
⅓ cup brewed coffee, at 80°F to 90°F
1½ tablespoons balsamic vinegar
1½ tablespoons olive oil
1½ tablespoons dark molasses
¾ tablespoon light brown sugar
¾ teaspoon salt
1½ teaspoons caraway seeds
3 tablespoons unsweetened cocoa powder
¾ cup dark rye flour
1¾ cups white bread flour
1½ teaspoons bread machine or instant yeast

Directions
1. **Preparing the Ingredients.**
   Place the ingredients in your bread maker as recommended by the manufacturer.
2. **Select the Bake cycle**
   Set the machine for Whole-Wheat/Whole-Grain bread, select light or medium crust, and press Start.
   When the bread is done, remove the bucket from the machine. Let the loaf cool for 5 minutes. Gently shake the bucket to remove the loaf, and turn it out onto a rack to cool.

Apple Cider Bread
PREP: 10 MINUTES PLUS FERMENTING TIME /MAKES 1 LOAF

Ingredients
8 slices bread (1 pound)
¼ cup milk, at 80°F to 90°F
2 tablespoons apple cider, at room temperature
2 tablespoons sugar
4 teaspoons melted butter, cooled
1 tablespoon honey
¼ teaspoon salt
2 cups white bread flour
¾ teaspoons bread machine or instant yeast
⅔ apple, peeled, cored, and finely diced

Directions
1. **Preparing the Ingredients.**
   Place the ingredients, except the apple, in your bread machine as recommended by the manufacturer.
2. **Select the Bake cycle**
   Set the machine for Basic/White bread, select light or medium crust, and press Start.
   Add the apple when the machine signals or 5 minutes before the last kneading cycle is complete.
   When the cycle is finished, remove the pan from the Cuisinart Bread Machine and let it rest.
   Take the bread out, put in a wire rack to Cool about 5 minutes. Slice

Sweet Pineapple Bread

PREP: 10 MINUTES PLUS FERMENTING TIME /MAKES 1 LOAF

Ingredients
16 slice bread (2 pounds)
6 tablespoons unsalted butter, melted
2 eggs, at room temperature
½ cup coconut milk, at room temperature
½ cup pineapple juice, at room temperature
1 cup sugar
1½ teaspoons coconut extract
2 cups all-purpose flour
¾ cup shredded sweetened coconut
1 teaspoon baking powder
½ teaspoon table salt

Directions
1. **Preparing the Ingredients.**
   Place the ingredients, except the apple, in your bread machine as recommended by the manufacturer.
2. **Select the Bake cycle**
   Set the machine for Quick/Rapid bread, select light or medium crust, and press Start.
   Add the apple when the machine signals or 5 minutes before the last kneading cycle is complete.
   When the cycle is finished, remove the pan from the Cuisinart Bread Machine and let it rest.
   Take the bread out, put in a wire rack to Cool about 5 minutes. Slice

Coffee Cake
PREP: 10 MINUTES PLUS FERMENTING TIME /MAKES 1 LOAF

Ingredients
12 to 16 slice bread (1½ to 2 pounds)
¾ cup buttermilk, at room temperature
¾ cup (1½ sticks) butter, at room temperature
1 tablespoon instant coffee granules
3 eggs, at room temperature
¾ cup sugar
2 cups all-purpose flour
½ tablespoon baking powder
½ teaspoon salt
1 cup chopped pecans

Directions
1. **Preparing the Ingredients.**
   Place the buttermilk, butter, coffee granules, eggs, and sugar in the bread maker.
2. **Select the Bake cycle**
   Set the machine for Quick/Rapid bread and press Start. While the wet ingredients are mixing, stir together the flour, baking powder, salt, and pecans in a small bowl. After the first fast mixing is done, add the dry ingredients. When the cycle is finished, remove the pan from the Cuisinart Bread Machine and let it rest.
   Take the bread out, put in a wire rack to Cool about 5 minutes. Slice

Caramel Apple and Pecan Bread
PREP: 10 MINUTES PLUS FERMENTING TIME /MAKES 1 LOAF

Ingredients
12 slice bread (1½ pounds)
1 cup water
2 tablespoons butter, softened
3 cups bread flour
¼ cup packed brown sugar
¾ teaspoon ground cinnamon
1 teaspoon salt
2 teaspoons bread machine or fast-acting dry yeast
½ cup chopped unpeeled apple
1/3 cup coarsely chopped pecans, toasted

Directions
1. **Preparing the Ingredients.**
   Choose the size of loaf of your preference and then measure the ingredients.
   Add all of the ingredients mentioned previously in the list except apple and pecans in bread maker. Add apple and pecans at the Raisin/Nut signal or 5 to 10 minutes before last kneading cycle ends.
2. **Select the Bake cycle**
   Set the machine for Basic/White bread and press Start.
   When the cycle is finished, remove the pan from the Cuisinart Bread Machine and let it rest.
   Take the bread out, put in a wire rack to Cool about 5 minutes. Slice

Cocoa Banana Bread
PREP: 10 MINUTES PLUS FERMENTING TIME /MAKES 1 LOAF

Ingredients
12 slice bread (1½ pounds)
3 bananas, mashed
2 eggs, at room temperature
¾ cup packed light brown sugar
½ cup unsalted butter, melted
½ cup sour cream, at room temperature
¼ cup sugar
1½ teaspoons pure vanilla extract
1 cup all-purpose flour
½ cup quick oats
2 tablespoons unsweetened cocoa powder
1 teaspoon baking soda

Directions
1. **Preparing the Ingredients.**
   Choose the size of loaf of your preference and then measure the ingredients.
   Add all of the ingredients mentioned previously in the list.
   Close after placing the pan in the Cuisinart Bread Machine.
2. **Select the Bake cycle**
   Turn on the Cuisinart Bread Machine. Select the Quick/Rapid setting, select the loaf size, and the crust color. Press start.
   When the cycle is finished, remove the pan from the Cuisinart Bread Machine and let it rest.
   Take the bread out, put in a wire rack to Cool about 5 minutes. Slice

Pumpkin Coconut Bread
PREP: 10 MINUTES PLUS FERMENTING TIME /MAKES 1 LOAF

Ingredients
12 to 16 slice bread (1½ to 2 pounds)
1 cup pure canned pumpkin
½ cup (1 stick) butter, at room temperature
1½ teaspoons pure vanilla extract
1 cup sugar
½ cup dark brown sugar
2 cups all-purpose flour
¾ cup sweetened shredded coconut
1½ teaspoons ground cinnamon
1 teaspoon baking soda
1 teaspoon baking powder
½ teaspoon ground nutmeg
½ teaspoon ground ginger
⅛ teaspoon ground allspice

Directions
1. **Preparing the Ingredients.**
   Place the pumpkin, butter, vanilla, sugar, and dark brown sugar in your bread machine.
2. **Select the Bake cycle**
   Set the machine for Quick/Rapid bread and press Start.
   After the first fast mixing is done, add the flour, coconut, cinnamon, baking soda, baking powder, nutmeg, ginger, and allspice.
   When the cycle is finished, remove the pan from the Cuisinart Bread Machine and let it rest.
   Take the bread out, put in a wire rack to Cool about 5 minutes. Slice.

Cranberry-Cornmeal Bread
PREP: 10 MINUTES PLUS FERMENTING TIME /MAKES 1 LOAF

Ingredients
12 slice bread (1½ pounds)
1 cup plus 1 tablespoon water
3 tablespoons molasses or honey
2 tablespoons butter, softened
3 cups bread flour
1/3 cup cornmeal
1½ teaspoons salt
2 teaspoons bread machine yeast
½ cup sweetened dried cranberries

Directions
1. **Preparing the Ingredients.**
   Choose the size of loaf of your preference and then measure the ingredients.
   Add all of the ingredients mentioned previously in the list except cranberries
   Close after placing the pan in the Cuisinart Bread Machine.
   Add cranberries at the Raisin/Nut signal or 5 to 10 minutes before last kneading cycle ends.
2. **Select the Bake cycle**
   Set the machine for White/Basic bread and press Start.
   After the first fast mixing is done, add the flour, coconut, cinnamon, baking soda, baking powder, nutmeg, ginger, and allspice. When the cycle is finished, remove the pan from the Cuisinart Bread Machine and let it rest.
   Take the bread out, put in a wire rack to Cool about 5 minutes. Slice.

Coconut Delight Bread
PREP: 10 MINUTES PLUS FERMENTING TIME /MAKES 1 LOAF

Ingredients
16 slice bread (2 pounds)
1⅓ cups lukewarm milk
1 egg, at room temperature
2 tablespoons unsalted butter, melted
2⅔ teaspoons pure coconut extract
3⅓ tablespoons sugar
1 teaspoon table salt
⅔ cup sweetened shredded coconut
4 cups white bread flour
2 teaspoons bread machine yeast

Directions
1. **Preparing the Ingredients.**
   Choose the size of loaf of your preference and then measure the ingredients.
   Add all of the ingredients mentioned previously in the list.
   Close after placing the pan in the Cuisinart Bread Machine.
2. **Select the Bake cycle**
   Turn on the Cuisinart Bread Machine. Select the Sweet setting, select the loaf size, and the crust color. Press start.
   When the cycle is finished, remove the pan from the Cuisinart Bread Machine and let it rest.
   Take the bread out, put in a wire rack to Cool about 5 minutes. Slice

Vanilla Almond Milk Bread
PREP: 10 MINUTES PLUS FERMENTING TIME /MAKES 1 LOAF

Ingredients

12 slice bread (1½ pounds)
½ cup plus 1 tablespoon milk, at 80°F to 90°F
3 tablespoons melted butter, cooled
3 tablespoons sugar
1 egg, at room temperature
1½ teaspoons pure vanilla extract
⅓ teaspoon almond extract
2½ cups white bread flour
1½ teaspoons bread machine or instant yeast

Directions

1. **Preparing the Ingredients.**
   Choose the size of loaf of your preference and then measure the ingredients.
   Add all of the ingredients mentioned previously in the list.
   Close after placing the pan in the Cuisinart Bread Machine.
2. **Select the Bake cycle**
   Turn on the Cuisinart Bread Machine. Select the Sweet setting, select the loaf size, and the crust color. Press start.
   When the cycle is finished, remove the pan from the Cuisinart Bread Machine and let it rest.
   Take the bread out, put in a wire rack to Cool about 5 minutes. Slice

Chocolate Chip Bread
PREP: 10 MINUTES PLUS FERMENTING TIME /MAKES 1 LOAF

Ingredients

12 slice bread (1½ pounds)
1 cup sour cream
2 eggs, at room temperature
1 cup sugar
½ cup unsalted butter, melted
¼ cup plain Greek yogurt
1¾ cups all-purpose flour
½ cup unsweetened cocoa powder
½ teaspoon baking powder
½ teaspoon table salt
1 cup milk chocolate chips

Directions

3. **Preparing the Ingredients.**
   Choose the size of loaf of your preference and then measure the ingredients.
   Add all of the ingredients mentioned previously in the list.
   Close after placing the pan in the Cuisinart Bread Machine.
4. **Select the Bake cycle**
   Turn on the Cuisinart Bread Machine. Select the Quick/Rapid setting, select the loaf size, and the crust color. Press start.
   When the cycle is finished, remove the pan from the Cuisinart Bread Machine and let it rest.
   Take the bread out, put in a wire rack to Cool about 5 minutes. Slice

Triple Chocolate Bread

PREP: 10 MINUTES PLUS FERMENTING TIME / MAKES 1 LOAF

Ingredients

8 slices bread (1 pound)
⅔ cup milk, at 80°F to 90°F
1 egg, at room temperature
1½ tablespoons melted butter, cooled
1 teaspoon pure vanilla extract
2 tablespoons light brown sugar
1 tablespoon unsweetened cocoa powder
½ teaspoon salt
2 cups white bread flour
1 teaspoon bread machine or instant yeast
¼ cup semisweet chocolate chips
¼ cup white chocolate chips

Directions

1. **Preparing the Ingredients.**
   Place the ingredients, except the chocolate chips, in your bread machine as recommended by the manufacturer.
2. **Select the Bake cycle**
   Set the machine for Basic/White bread, select light or medium crust, and press Start.
   When the machine signals, add the chocolate chips, or put them in the nut/raisin hopper and the machine will add them automatically.
   When the bread is done, remove the bucket from the machine.
   Let the loaf cool for 5 minutes.
   Gently shake the bucket to remove the loaf, and turn it out onto a rack to cool.

Sweet Vanilla Bread
PREP: 10 MINUTES PLUS FERMENTING TIME /MAKES 1 LOAF

Ingredients
12 slice bread (1½ pounds)
½ cup + 1 tablespoon lukewarm milk
3 tablespoons unsalted butter, melted
3 tablespoons sugar
1 egg, at room temperature
1½ teaspoons pure vanilla extract
⅓ teaspoon almond extract
2½ cups white bread flour
1½ teaspoons bread machine yeast

Directions
1. **Preparing the Ingredients.**
   Choose the size of loaf you would like to make and measure your ingredients.
   Add the ingredients to the bread pan in the order listed above.
   Insert the bread pan in the Cuisinart Bread Machine.

2. **Select the Bake cycle**
   Press the "Start" button. Select the White/Basic setting, then the loaf size, and finally the crust color. Start the cycle.
   When the cycle is finished, remove the pan from the bread maker. Let rest for a few minutes.
   Take the bread out and allow to cool on a wire rack for at least 10 minutes before slicing.

Chocolate Oatmeal Banana Bread
PREP: 10 MINUTES PLUS FERMENTING TIME /MAKES 1 LOAF

Ingredients
12 to 16 slice bread (1½ to 2 pounds)
3 bananas, mashed
2 eggs, at room temperature
¾ cup packed light brown sugar
½ cup (1 stick) butter, at room temperature
½ cup sour cream, at room temperature
¼ cup sugar
1½ teaspoons pure vanilla extract
1 cup all-purpose flour
½ cup quick oats
2 tablespoons unsweetened cocoa powder
1 teaspoon baking soda

Directions
1. **Preparing the Ingredients.**
   Place the banana, eggs, brown sugar, butter, sour cream, sugar, and vanilla in your bread machine.
   Set the machine for Quick/Rapid bread and press Start.
   While the wet ingredients are mixing, stir together the flour, oats, cocoa powder, and baking soda in a small bowl.

2. **Select the Bake cycle**
   After the first fast mixing is done, add the dry ingredients.
   When the bread is done, remove the bucket from the machine.
   Let the loaf cool for 5 minutes.
   Gently shake the bucket to remove the loaf, and turn it out onto a rack to cool.

SPECIALTY BREAD

Festive Raspberry Rolls
PREP: 10 MINUTES PLUS FERMENTING TIME /MAKES 12 ROLLS

Ingredients
1/3 cup milk
1/3 cup water
3 tablespoons butter, softened
1 egg
2 cups bread flour
1/3 cup sugar
½ teaspoon salt
1¾ teaspoons bread machine or fast-acting dry yeast
3 tablespoons raspberry preserves

Directions
1. **Preparing the Ingredients.**
   Measure carefully, placing all ingredients except preserves in bread machine pan in the order recommended by the manufacturer.
2. **Select the Bake cycle**
   Select Dough/Manual cycle. Do not use delay cycle.
   Remove dough from pan, using lightly floured hands. Cover and let rest 10 minutes on lightly floured surface.
   Grease 12 regular-size muffin cups. Roll or pat dough into 15×10-inch rectangle. Spread preserves over dough to within ¼ inch of edges. Starting with 15-inch side, roll up dough; pinch edge of dough into roll to seal. Stretch and shape roll to make even.
   Cut roll into 12 equal slices. Place slices, cut side up, in muffin cups. Using kitchen scissors, snip through each slice twice, cutting into fourths. Gently spread dough pieces open. Cover and let rise in warm place about 25 minutes or until doubled in size. Dough is ready if indentation remains when touched. Heat oven to 375°F. Bake 15 to 20 minutes or until golden brown.
   Immediately remove from pan to cooling rack. Serve warm or cool.

Italian Easter Cake
PREP: 10 MINUTES PLUS FERMENTING TIME /MAKES 4 SLICES

Ingredients
1¾ cups wheat flour
2½ Tbsp quick-acting dry yeast
8 Tbsp sugar
½ tsp salt
3 chicken eggs
¾ cup milk
3 Tbsp butter
1 cup raisins

Directions
1. **Preparing the Ingredients**
   Add each ingredient except the raisins to the Cuisinart Bread Machine in the order and at the temperature recommended by your bread machine manufacturer.
2. **Select the Bake cycle**
   Close, select the sweet loaf, low crust setting on your bread machine, and press start.
   When the Cuisinart Bread Machine has finished baking, remove the bread and put it on a cooling rack.

Eggnog Bread

PREP: 10 MINUTES PLUS FERMENTING TIME /MAKES 1 LOAF

Ingredients
8 slice bread (1 pounds)
¾ cup eggnog, at 80°F to 90°F
¾ tablespoon melted butter, cooled
1 tablespoon sugar
⅔ teaspoon salt
¼ teaspoon ground cinnamon
¼ teaspoon ground nutmeg
2 cups white bread flour
¾ teaspoon bread machine or instant yeast

Directions
1. **Preparing the Ingredients.**
   Choose the size of loaf of your preference and then measure the ingredients
   Add all of the ingredients mentioned previously in the list except.
   Close after placing the pan in the Cuisinart Bread Machine.
2. **Select the Bake cycle**
   Press the "Start" button. Select the White/Basic setting, then the loaf size, and finally the crust color. Start the cycle.
   When the cycle is finished, remove the pan from the Cuisinart Bread Machine and let it rest. Take the bread out, put in a wire rack to Cool about 10 minutes. Slice

Basil Pizza Dough

Ingredients
12 slice bread (1½ pounds)
1 cup lukewarm water
3 tablespoons olive oil
1 teaspoon table salt
1½ teaspoons sugar
1½ teaspoons basil, dried
3 cups white bread flour or all-purpose flour
1½ teaspoons bread machine yeast

Directions
1. **Preparing the Ingredients.**
   Choose the size of loaf of your preference and then measure the ingredients
   Add all of the ingredients mentioned previously in the list.
   Close after placing the pan in the Cuisinart Bread Machine.
2. **Select the Bake cycle**
   Press the "Start" button. Select the Dough setting and then the dough size. Press start.
   When the cycle is finished, carefully remove the dough from the pan.
   Place the dough on a floured surface and roll to make a pizza crust of your desired thickness. Set aside for 15 minutes.
   Top with your favorite pizza sauce, toppings and cheese.
   Bake in an oven at 400°F or 204°C for 20 minutes or until the edges turn lightly golden.

Whole-Wheat Challah
PREP: 10 MINUTES PLUS FERMENTING TIME /MAKES 1 LOAF

Ingredients
12 slice bread (1½ pounds)
¾ cup water, at 80°F to 90°F
⅓ cup melted butter, cooled
2 eggs, at room temperature
1½ teaspoons salt
3 tablespoons sugar
1 cup whole-wheat flour
2 cups white bread flour
1⅔ teaspoons bread machine or instant yeast

Directions
1. **Preparing the Ingredients.**
   Choose the size of loaf of your preference and then measure the ingredients.
   Add all of the ingredients mentioned previously in the list.
   Close after placing the pan in the Cuisinart Bread Machine.
2. **Select the Bake cycle**
   Turn on the Cuisinart Bread Machine. Select Whole Wheat setting, select the loaf size, and the crust color. Press start.
   When the cycle is finished, remove the pan from the Cuisinart Bread Machine and let it rest.
   Take the bread out, put in a wire rack to Cool about 10 minutes. Slice

Classic Sourdough Bread
PREP: 10 MINUTES PLUS FERMENTING TIME /MAKES 1 LOAF

Ingredients
12 slice bread (1½ pounds)
2 tablespoons lukewarm water
2 cups sourdough starter
2 tablespoons unsalted butter, melted
2 teaspoons sugar
1½ teaspoons salt
2½ cups white bread flour
1½ teaspoons bread machine yeast
Sourdough Starter
2 cups lukewarm water
2 cups all-purpose flour
2½ teaspoons bread machine yeast

Directions
1. **Preparing the Ingredients.**
   Add the water, flour, and yeast to a medium-size non-metallic bowl. Mix well until no lumps are visible.
   Cover the bowl loosely and leave it in a warm area of your kitchen for 5–8 days. Do not place in a fridge or under direct sunlight.
   Stir the mixture several times every day. Always put the cover back on the bowl afterward.
   The starter is ready to use when it appears bubbly and has a sour smell.
   Choose the size of loaf of your preference and then measure the ingredients. Add all of the ingredients mentioned previously in the list. Close after placing the pan in the Cuisinart Bread Machine.
2. **Select the Bake cycle**
   Turn on the Cuisinart Bread Machine. Select Whole Wheat setting, select the loaf size, and the crust color. Press start.
   When the cycle is finished, remove the pan from the Cuisinart Bread Machine and let it rest. Take the bread out, put in a wire rack to Cool about 10 minutes. Slice

Portuguese Sweet Bread
PREP: 10 MINUTES PLUS FERMENTING TIME /MAKES 1 LOAF

Ingredients

8 slice bread (1 pound)
⅔ cup milk, at 80°F to 90°F
1 egg, at room temperature
4 teaspoons butter, softened
⅓ cup sugar
⅔ teaspoon salt
2 cups white bread flour
1½ teaspoons bread machine or instant yeast

Directions
1. **Preparing the Ingredients.**
    Choose the size of loaf of your preference and then measure the ingredients.
    Add all of the ingredients mentioned previously in the list.
    Close after placing the pan in the Cuisinart Bread Machine.
2. **Select the Bake cycle**
    Turn on the Cuisinart Bread Machine. Select Sweet setting, select the loaf size, and the crust color. Press start.
    When the cycle is finished, remove the pan from the Cuisinart Bread Machine and let it rest.
    Take the bread out, put in a wire rack to Cool about 10 minutes. Slice

Milk Honey Sourdough Bread
PREP: 10 MINUTES PLUS FERMENTING TIME /MAKES 1 LOAF

Ingredients

16 slice bread (2 pounds)
½ cup lukewarm milk
2 cups sourdough starter
¼ cup olive oil
2 tablespoons honey
1⅓ teaspoons salt
4 cups white bread flour
1⅓ teaspoons bread machine yeast

Directions
1. **Preparing the Ingredients.**
    Choose the size of loaf of your preference and then measure the ingredients.
    Add all of the ingredients mentioned previously in the list.
    Close after placing the pan in the Cuisinart Bread Machine.
2. **Select the Bake cycle**
    Turn on the Cuisinart Bread Machine. Select White/ Basic setting, select the loaf size, and the crust color. Press start.
    When the cycle is finished, remove the pan from the Cuisinart Bread Machine and let it rest.
    Take the bread out, put in a wire rack to Cool about 10 minutes. Slice

Pecan Maple Bread
PREP: 10 MINUTES PLUS FERMENTING TIME / MAKES 1 LOAF

Ingredients
16 slice bread (2 pounds)
1½ cups (3 sticks) butter, at room temperature
4 eggs, at room temperature
⅔ cup maple syrup
⅔ cup sugar
3 cups all-purpose flour
1 cup chopped pecans
2 teaspoons baking powder
½ teaspoon salt

Directions
1. **Preparing the Ingredients.**
   Place the butter, eggs, maple syrup, and sugar in your bread machine.
2. **Select the Bake cycle**
   Set the machine for Quick/Rapid bread and press Start. While the wet ingredients are mixing, stir together the flour, pecans, baking powder, and salt in a small bowl. After the first fast mixing is done, add the dry ingredients. When the cycle is finished, remove the pan from the Cuisinart Bread Machine and let it rest.
   Take the bread out, put in a wire rack to Cool about 10 minutes. Slice

Cherry Christmas Bread
PREP: 10 MINUTES PLUS FERMENTING TIME / MAKES 1 LOAF

Ingredients
16 slice bread (2 pounds)
1 cup + 1 tablespoon lukewarm milk
1 egg, at room temperature
2 tablespoons unsalted butter, melted
3 tablespoons light brown sugar
⅛ teaspoon ground cinnamon
4 cups white bread flour, divided
1½ teaspoons bread machine yeast
⅔ cup candied cherries
½ cup chopped almonds
½ cup raisins, chopped

Directions
1. **Preparing the Ingredients.**
   Choose the size of loaf you would like to make and measure your ingredients.
   Add all of the ingredients except for the cherries, raisins, and almonds to the bread pan in the order listed above.
   Close after placing the pan in the Cuisinart Bread Machine.
2. **Select the Bake cycle**
   Turn on the Cuisinart Bread Machine. Select the White/Basic or Fruit/Nut (if your machine has this setting) setting, then the loaf size, and finally the crust color. Press start
   When the machine signals to add ingredients, add the cherries, raisins, and almonds.
   When the cycle is finished, remove the pan from the Cuisinart Bread Machine and let it rest. Take the bread out, put in a wire rack to Cool about 10 minutes. Slice

Nana's Gingerbread
PREP: 10 MINUTES PLUS FERMENTING TIME /MAKES 1 LOAF

Ingredients
8 slice bread (1 pound)
⅔ cup buttermilk, at 80°F to 90°F
1 egg, at room temperature
2⅔ tablespoons dark molasses
2 teaspoons melted butter, cooled
2 tablespoons sugar
1 teaspoon salt
1 teaspoon ground ginger
⅔ teaspoon ground cinnamon
⅓ teaspoon ground nutmeg
⅛ teaspoon ground cloves
2⅓ cups white bread flour
1⅓ teaspoons bread machine or active dry yeast

Directions
1. **Preparing the Ingredients.**
   Place the ingredients in your bread maker as recommended by the manufacturer.
2. **Select the Bake cycle**
   Set the machine for Sweet bread and press Start. When the cycle is finished, remove the pan from the Cuisinart Bread Machine and let it rest. Take the bread out, put in a wire rack to Cool about 10 minutes. Slice

Coffee Caraway Seed Bread
PREP: 10 MINUTES PLUS FERMENTING TIME /MAKES 1 LOAF

Ingredients
12 slice bread (1½ pounds)
¾ cup lukewarm water
⅓ cup brewed coffee, lukewarm
1½ tablespoons balsamic vinegar
1½ tablespoons olive oil
1½ tablespoons dark molasses
¾ tablespoon light brown sugar
¾ teaspoon table salt
1½ teaspoons caraway seeds
3 tablespoons unsweetened cocoa powder
¾ cup dark rye flour
1¾ cups white bread flour
1½ teaspoons bread machine yeast

Directions
1. **Preparing the Ingredients.**
   Choose the size of loaf of your preference and then measure the ingredients.
   Add all of the ingredients mentioned previously in the list.
   Close after placing the pan in the Cuisinart Bread Machine.
2. **Select the Bake cycle**
   Turn on the Cuisinart Bread Machine. Select Whole wheat/ Wholegrain setting, select the loaf size, and the crust color. Press start.
   When the cycle is finished, remove the pan from the Cuisinart Bread Machine and let it rest.
   Take the bread out, put in a wire rack to Cool about 10 minutes. Slice

Bread Machine Brioche
PREP: 10 MINUTES PLUS FERMENTING TIME /MAKES 1 LOAF

Ingredients

12 slice bread (1½ pounds)
½ cup plus 1 tablespoon milk, at 80°F to 90°F
3 eggs, at room temperature
2 tablespoons sugar
¾ teaspoon salt
3 cups white bread flour
1½ teaspoons bread machine or instant yeast
½ cup (1 stick) butter, softened

Directions
1. **Preparing the Ingredients.**
   Choose the size of loaf of your preference and then measure the ingredients.
   Add all of the ingredients mentioned previously in the list.
   Close after placing the pan in the Cuisinart Bread Machine.
2. **Select the Bake cycle**
   Turn on the Cuisinart Bread Machine. Select White/ Basic setting, select the loaf size, and the crust color. Press start.
   When the cycle is finished, remove the pan from the Cuisinart Bread Machine and let it rest.
   Take the bread out, put in a wire rack to Cool about 10 minutes. Slice

Sun-Dried Tomato Rolls
PREP: 10 MINUTES PLUS FERMENTING TIME /MAKES 12 ROLLS

Ingredients

¾ cup warm milk (105°F to 115°F)
2 cups bread flour
¼ cup chopped sun-dried tomatoes in oil, drained, 1 tablespoon oil reserved 1 tablespoon sugar
1 teaspoon salt
1½ teaspoons bread machine yeast

Directions
1. **Preparing the Ingredients.**
   Measure carefully, placing all ingredients in bread machine pan in the order recommended by the manufacturer.
2. **Select the Bake cycle**
   Select Dough/Manual cycle. Do not use delay cycle.
   Remove dough from pan; place on lightly floured surface. Cover and let rest 10 minutes Lightly grease cookie sheet with shortening or spray with cooking spray.
   Gently push fist into dough to deflate. Divide dough into 12 equal pieces. Shape each piece into a ball. Place balls about 2 inches apart on cookie sheet. Cover and let rise in warm place 30 to 45 minutes or until almost doubled in size.
   Heat oven to 350°F. Bake 12 to 16 minutes or until golden brown. Remove from cookie sheet to cooling rack. Serve warm or cool.

Cinnamon Beer Bread
PREP: 10 MINUTES PLUS FERMENTING TIME /MAKES 1 LOAF

Ingredients

16 slice bread (2 pounds)
2 cups beer, at room temperature
1 cup unsalted butter, melted
⅓ cup honey
4 cups all-purpose flour
1⅓ teaspoons table salt
⅓ teaspoon ground cinnamon
1⅓ tablespoons baking powder

Directions
1. **Preparing the Ingredients.**
   Choose the size of loaf of your preference and then measure the ingredients.
   Add all of the ingredients mentioned previously in the list.
   Close after placing the pan in the Cuisinart Bread Machine.
2. **Select the Bake cycle**
   Turn on the Cuisinart Bread Machine. Select Quick/ Rapid setting, select the loaf size, and the crust color. Press start.
   When the cycle is finished, remove the pan from the Cuisinart Bread Machine and let it rest.
   Take the bread out, put in a wire rack to Cool about 10 minutes. Slice

Traditional Paska
PREP: 10 MINUTES PLUS FERMENTING TIME /MAKES 1 LOAF

Ingredients

12 slice bread (1½ pounds)
¾ cup milk, at 80°F to 90°F
2 eggs, at room temperature
2 tablespoons butter, melted and cooled
¼ cup sugar
1 teaspoon salt
2 teaspoons lemon zest
3 cups white bread flour
2 teaspoons bread machine or instant yeast

Directions
1. **Preparing the Ingredients.**
   Choose the size of loaf of your preference and then measure the ingredients.
   Add all of the ingredients mentioned previously in the list.
   Close after placing the pan in the Cuisinart Bread Machine.
2. **Select the Bake cycle**
   Turn on the Cuisinart Bread Machine. Select Basic/ White setting, select the loaf size, and the crust color. Press start.
   When the cycle is finished, remove the pan from the Cuisinart Bread Machine and let it rest.
   Take the bread out, put in a wire rack to Cool about 10 minutes. Slice

French Butter Bread
PREP: 10 MINUTES PLUS FERMENTING TIME /MAKES 1 LOAF

Ingredients
12 slice bread (1½ pounds)
½ cup + 1 tablespoon lukewarm milk
3 eggs, at room temperature
2 tablespoons sugar
¾ teaspoon table salt
½ cup unsalted butter, melted
3 cups white bread flour
1½ teaspoons bread machine yeast

Directions
1. **Preparing the Ingredients.**
   Choose the size of loaf of your preference and then measure the ingredients.
   Add all of the ingredients mentioned previously in the list.
   Close after placing the pan in the Cuisinart Bread Machine.
2. **Select the Bake cycle**
   Set the machine for Basic / White bread and press Start.
   About 10 minutes before the end of your first kneading cycle, begin adding the butter, 1 tablespoon each minute.
   When the cycle is finished, remove the pan from the Cuisinart Bread Machine and let it rest.
   Take the bread out, put in a wire rack to Cool about 10 minutes.

Raisin and Nut Paska
PREP: 10 MINUTES PLUS FERMENTING TIME /MAKES 1 LOAF

Ingredients
12 slice bread (1½ pounds)
¾ cup milk, at 80°F to 90°F
2 eggs, at room temperature
2 tablespoons butter, melted and cooled
¼ cup sugar
1 teaspoon salt
2 teaspoons lemon zest
3 cups white bread flour
2 teaspoons bread machine or instant yeast
⅓ cup slivered almonds
⅓ cup golden raisins

Directions
1. **Preparing the Ingredients.**
   Place the ingredients, except the almonds and raisins, in your bread machine as recommended by the manufacturer.
2. **Select the Bake cycle**
   Set the machine for Basic/White bread, select light or medium crust, and press Start.
   When the bread is done, remove the bucket from the machine.
   Add the almonds and raisins when the machine signals or 5 minutes before the second kneading cycle is finished.
   When the cycle is finished, remove the pan from the Cuisinart Bread Machine and let it rest.
   Take the bread out, put in a wire rack to Cool about 10 minutes

Holiday Chocolate Bread
PREP: 10 MINUTES PLUS FERMENTING TIME /MAKES 1 LOAF

Ingredients
12 slice bread (1½ pounds)
⅞ cup lukewarm milk
1 egg, at room temperature
1½ tablespoons unsalted butter, melted
1 teaspoon pure vanilla extract
2 tablespoons sugar
¾ teaspoon table salt
3 cups white bread flour
1 teaspoon bread machine yeast
½ cup white chocolate chips
⅓ cup dried cranberries

Directions
1. **Preparing the Ingredients.**
   Choose the size of loaf of your preference and then measure the ingredients.
   Add all of the ingredients mentioned previously in the list except for the chocolate chips and cranberries to the bread pan in the order listed above.
   Close after placing the pan in the Cuisinart Bread Machine.
2. **Select the Bake cycle**
   Press the "Start" button. Select the White/Basic or Fruit/Nut (if your machine has this setting) setting, then the loaf size, and finally the crust color. Start the cycle. When the machine signals to add ingredients, add the chocolate chips and cranberries. When the cycle is finished, remove the pan from the Cuisinart Bread Machine and let it rest.
   Take the bread out, put in a wire rack to Cool about 10 minutes

Honey Cake
PREP: 10 MINUTES PLUS FERMENTING TIME /MAKES 1 LOAF

Ingredients
12 to 16 slice bread (1½ to 2 pounds)
⅓ cup brewed coffee, cooled to room temperature
½ cup (1 stick) butter, melted and cooled
½ cup honey
¾ cup sugar
¼ cup dark brown sugar
2 eggs, at room temperature
2 tablespoons whiskey
¼ cup freshly squeezed orange juice, at room temperature
1 teaspoon pure vanilla extract
2 cups all-purpose flour
½ tablespoon baking powder
½ tablespoon ground cinnamon
½ teaspoon baking soda
¼ teaspoon ground allspice
¼ teaspoon salt
¼ teaspoon ground cloves

Directions
1. **Preparing the Ingredients.**
   Place the coffee, butter, honey, sugar, brown sugar, eggs, whiskey, orange juice, and vanilla in your bread machine.
2. **Select the Bake cycle**
   Set the machine for Quick/Rapid bread and press Start. While the wet ingredients are mixing, stir together the flour, baking powder, cinnamon, baking soda, allspice, salt, and cloves in a small bowl. After the first fast mixing is done, add the dry ingredients. When the cycle is finished, remove the pan from the Cuisinart Bread Machine and let it rest. Take the bread out, put in a wire rack to Cool about 10 minutes

New Year Spiced Bread
PREP: 10 MINUTES PLUS FERMENTING TIME /MAKES 1 LOAF

Ingredients
12 slice bread (1½ pounds)
⅓ cup brewed coffee, cooled to room temperature
½ cup unsalted butter, melted
½ cup honey
¾ cup sugar
¼ cup dark brown sugar
2 eggs, at room temperature
2 tablespoons whiskey
¼ cup orange juice, at room temperature
1 teaspoon pure vanilla extract
2 cups all-purpose flour
½ tablespoon ground cinnamon
½ teaspoon baking soda
¼ teaspoon ground allspice
¼ teaspoon table salt
¼ teaspoon ground cloves
½ tablespoon baking powder

Directions
1. **Preparing the Ingredients.**
   Choose the size of loaf of your preference and then measure the ingredients.
   Add all of the ingredients mentioned previously in the list.
   Close after placing the pan in the Cuisinart Bread Machine.
2. **Select the Bake cycle**
   Turn on the Cuisinart Bread Machine. Select Quick/ Rapid setting, select the loaf size, and the crust color. Press start.
   When the cycle is finished, remove the pan from the Cuisinart Bread Machine and let it rest.
   Take the bread out, put in a wire rack to Cool about 10 minutes. Slice

Christmas Fruit Bread
PREP: 10 MINUTES PLUS FERMENTING TIME /MAKES 1 LOAF

Ingredients
8 slice bread (1 pound)
¾ cup plus 1 tablespoon milk, at 80°F to 90°F
2⅔ tablespoons melted butter, cooled
⅓ teaspoon pure vanilla extract
⅛ teaspoon pure almond extract
2 tablespoons light brown sugar
⅔ teaspoon salt
1 teaspoon ground cinnamon
2 cups white bread flour
⅔ teaspoon bread machine or instant yeast
⅓ cup dried mixed fruit
⅓ cup golden raisins

Directions
1. **Preparing the Ingredients.**
   Place the ingredients, except the dried fruit and raisins, in your bread machine as recommended by the manufacturer.
2. **Select the Bake cycle**
   Set the machine for Basic/White bread, select light or medium crust, and press Start. Add the dried fruit and raisins when the machine signals or 5 minutes before the second kneading cycle is finished. When the cycle is finished, remove the pan from the Cuisinart Bread Machine and let it rest.
   Take the bread out, put in a wire rack to Cool about 10 minutes. Slice

Cocoa Holiday Bread
PREP: 10 MINUTES PLUS FERMENTING TIME / MAKES 1 LOAF

Ingredients
12 slice bread (1½ pounds)
¾ cup brewed coffee, lukewarm
⅓ cup evaporated milk, lukewarm
1½ tablespoons unsalted butter, melted
2¼ tablespoons honey
¾ tablespoon dark molasses
¾ tablespoon sugar
1 tablespoon unsweetened cocoa powder
¾ teaspoon table salt
1⅔ cups whole-wheat bread flour
1⅔ cups white bread flour
1⅔ teaspoons bread machine yeast

Directions
1. **Preparing the Ingredients.**
   Choose the size of loaf of your preference and then measure the ingredients.
   Add all of the ingredients mentioned previously in the list.
   Close after placing the pan in the Cuisinart Bread Machine.
2. **Select the Bake cycle**
   Turn on the Cuisinart Bread Machine. Select Sweet setting, select the loaf size, and the crust color. Press start.
   When the cycle is finished, remove the pan from the Cuisinart Bread Machine and let it rest.
   Take the bread out, put in a wire rack to Cool about 10 minutes. Slice

Stollen
PREP: 10 MINUTES PLUS FERMENTING TIME / MAKES 1 LOAF

Ingredients
12 slice bread (1½ pounds)
¾ cup milk, at 80°F to 90°F
1 egg, at room temperature
1½ tablespoons butter, melted and cooled
2¼ tablespoons light brown sugar
⅛ teaspoon ground cinnamon
3 cups white bread flour, divided
1⅛ teaspoons bread machine or instant yeast
½ cup red and green candied cherries
⅓ cup chopped almonds
⅓ cup raisins

Directions
1. **Preparing the Ingredients.**
   Place the ingredients, except the candied fruit, nuts, raisins, and ¼ cup of the flour, in your bread machine as recommended by the manufacturer.
2. **Select the Bake cycle**
   Set the machine for Basic/White bread, select light or medium crust, and press Start.
   In a small bowl, stir together the candied cherries, almonds, raisins, and ¼ cup of flour.
   Add the fruit and nut mixture when the machine signals or 5 minutes before the second kneading cycle is finished. When the cycle is finished, remove the pan from the Cuisinart Bread Machine and let it rest.
   Take the bread out, put in a wire rack to Cool about 10 minutes. Slice

Holiday Eggnog Bread
PREP: 10 MINUTES PLUS FERMENTING TIME / MAKES 1 LOAF

Ingredients
12 slice bread (1½ pounds)
1⅛ cups eggnog, at room temperature
1⅛ tablespoons unsalted butter, melted
1½ tablespoons sugar
1 teaspoon table salt
⅓ teaspoon ground cinnamon
⅓ teaspoon ground nutmeg
3 cups white bread flour
1⅓ teaspoons bread machine yeast

Directions
1. **Preparing the Ingredients.**
   Choose the size of loaf of your preference and then measure the ingredients.
   Add all of the ingredients mentioned previously in the list.
   Close after placing the pan in the Cuisinart Bread Machine.
2. **Select the Bake cycle**
   Turn on the Cuisinart Bread Machine. Select White / Basic setting, select the loaf size, and the crust color. Press start.
   When the cycle is finished, remove the pan from the Cuisinart Bread Machine and let it rest.
   Take the bread out, put in a wire rack to Cool about 10 minutes. Slice

Julekake
PREP: 10 MINUTES PLUS FERMENTING TIME / MAKES 1 LOAF

Ingredients
8 slice bread (1 pound)
⅔ cup milk, at 80°F to 90°F
1 egg, at room temperature
⅓ cup butter, melted and cooled
2⅔ tablespoons honey
⅓ teaspoon salt
⅓ teaspoon ground cardamom
¼ teaspoon ground cinnamon
2¼ cups white bread flour, plus 1 tablespoon
1½ teaspoons bread machine or instant yeast
⅓ cup golden raisins
⅓ cup candied citrus fruit
2⅔ tablespoons candied cherries

Directions
1. **Preparing the Ingredients.**
   Place the ingredients, except the raisins, candied citrus fruit, and 1 tablespoon of flour, in your bread machine as recommended by the manufacturer.
2. **Select the Bake cycle**
   Set the machine for Basic/White bread, select light or medium crust, and press Start.
   Toss the raisins, candied citrus fruit, and 1 tablespoon of flour together in a small bowl.
   Add the raisins, candied citrus fruit, and flour when the machine signals or 5 minutes before the second kneading cycle is finished. When the cycle is finished, remove the pan from the Cuisinart Bread Machine and let it rest.
   Take the bread out, put in a wire rack to Cool about 10 minutes. Slice

Easter Bread

PREP: 10 MINUTES PLUS FERMENTING TIME /MAKES 1 LOAF

Ingredients

16 slice bread (2 pounds)
1 cup lukewarm milk
2 eggs, at room temperature
2⅔ tablespoons unsalted butter, melted
⅓ cup sugar
1 teaspoon table salt
2⅓ teaspoons lemon zest
4 cups white bread flour
2¼ teaspoons bread machine yeast

Directions

1. **Preparing the Ingredients.**
   Choose the size of loaf of your preference and then measure the ingredients.
   Add all of the ingredients mentioned previously in the list.
   Close after placing the pan in the Cuisinart Bread Machine.
2. **Select the Bake cycle**
   Turn on the Cuisinart Bread Machine. Select White / Basic setting, select the loaf size, and the crust color. Press start.
   When the cycle is finished, remove the pan from the Cuisinart Bread Machine and let it rest.
   Take the bread out, put in a wire rack to Cool about 10 minutes. Slice

Spiked Eggnog Bread

PREP: 10 MINUTES PLUS FERMENTING TIME /MAKES 1 LOAF

Ingredients

12 to 16 slice bread (1½ to 2 pounds)
1 cup eggnog, at room temperature
1 cup sugar
2 eggs, at room temperature
½ cup (1 stick) butter, at room temperature
1 tablespoon dark rum
1½ teaspoons pure vanilla extract
½ teaspoon rum extract
2¼ cups all-purpose flour
2 teaspoons baking powder
¼ teaspoon ground cinnamon
½ teaspoon ground nutmeg
½ teaspoon salt

Directions

1. **Preparing the Ingredients.**
   Place the eggnog, sugar, eggs, butter, rum, vanilla, and rum extract in your bread machine.
2. **Select the Bake cycle**
   Set the machine for Quick/Rapid bread and press Start.
   While the wet ingredients are mixing, stir together the flour, baking powder, cinnamon, nutmeg, and salt in a small bowl.
   After the first fast mixing is done, add the dry ingredients. When the cycle is finished, remove the pan from the Cuisinart Bread Machine and let it rest. Take the bread out, put in a wire rack to Cool about 5 minutes. Slice

Hot Buttered Rum Bread
PREP: 10 MINUTES PLUS FERMENTING TIME /MAKES 1 LOAF

Ingredients
12 slice bread (1½ pounds)
¾ cup water, at 80°F to 90°F
1 egg, at room temperature
3 tablespoons butter, melted and cooled
3 tablespoons sugar
1 tablespoon rum extract
1¼ teaspoons salt
1 teaspoon ground cinnamon
¼ teaspoon ground nutmeg
3 cups white bread flour
1 teaspoon bread machine or instant yeast

Directions
3. **Preparing the Ingredients.**
   Choose the size of loaf of your preference and then measure the ingredients.
   Add all of the ingredients mentioned previously in the list.
   Close after placing the pan in the Cuisinart Bread Machine.
4. **Select the Bake cycle**
   Turn on the Cuisinart Bread Machine. Select Sweet setting, select the loaf size, and the crust color. Press start.
   When the cycle is finished, remove the pan from the Cuisinart Bread Machine and let it rest.
   Take the bread out, put in a wire rack to Cool about 10 minutes. Slice

Zucchini Pecan Bread
PREP: 10 MINUTES PLUS FERMENTING TIME /MAKES 1 LOAF

Ingredients
12 to 16 slice bread (1½ to 2 pounds)
2 eggs, at room temperature
½ cup melted butter, cooled
¾ cup shredded zucchini
½ cup packed light brown sugar
2 tablespoons sugar
1½ cups all-purpose flour
1 teaspoon ground cinnamon
½ teaspoon salt
½ teaspoon baking powder
½ teaspoon baking soda
¼ teaspoon ground allspice
½ cup chopped pecans

Directions
1. **Preparing the Ingredients.**
   Choose the size of loaf of your preference and then measure the ingredients.
   Add all of the ingredients mentioned previously in the list.
   Close after placing the pan in the Cuisinart Bread Machine.
2. **Select the Bake cycle**
   Turn on the Cuisinart Bread Machine. Select Quick/ Rapid setting, select the loaf size, and the crust color. Press start.
   When the cycle is finished, remove the pan from the Cuisinart Bread Machine and let it rest.
   Take the bread out, put in a wire rack to Cool about 10 minutes. Slice

About the Author

Amanda is a New York-based food writer, experienced chef. She loves sharing Easy, Delicious and Healthy Bread Machine recipes. Amanda is a passionate advocate for the Gluten Free lifestyle. When she's not cooking, Amanda enjoys spending time with her husband and her kids, gardening and traveling.

Made in the USA
Thornton, CO
04/22/22 09:09:43

0bf00419-ce2b-4c25-ad3a-7573239d32ebR01